Principles
in Practice

M000250028

The Principles in Practice imprint offers teachers concrete illustrations of effective classroom practices based in NCTE research briefs and policy statements. Each book discusses the research on a specific topic, links the research to an NCTE brief or policy statement, and then demonstrates how those principles come alive in practice: by showcasing actual classroom practices that demonstrate the policies in action; by talking about research in practical, teacher-friendly language; and by offering teachers possibilities for rethinking their own practices in light of the ideas presented in the books. Books within the imprint are grouped in strands, each strand focused on a significant topic of interest.

Adolescent Literacy Strand

Adolescent Literacy at Risk? The Impact of Standards (2009) Rebecca Bowers Sipe

Adolescents and Digital Literacies: Learning Alongside Our Students (2010) Sara Kajder

Adolescent Literacy and the Teaching of Reading: Lessons for Teachers of Literature (2010) Deborah Appleman

Writing in Today's Classrooms Strand

Writing in the Dialogical Classroom: Students and Teachers Responding to the Texts of Their Lives (2011) Bob Fecho

Becoming Writers in the Elementary Classroom: Visions and Decisions (2011) Katie Van Sluys

Writing Instruction in the Culturally Relevant Classroom (2011) Maisha T. Winn and Latrise P. Johnson

Literacy Assessment Strand

Our Better Judgment: Teacher Leadership for Writing Assessment (2012) Chris W. Gallagher and Eric D. Turley

Beyond Standardized Truth: Improving Teaching and Learning through Inquiry-Based Reading Assessment (2012) Scott Filkins

Reading Assessment: Artful Teachers, Successful Students (2013) Diane Stephens, editor

Literacies of the Disciplines Strand

Entering the Conversations: Practicing Literacy in the Disciplines (2014) Patricia Lambert Stock, Trace Schillinger, and Andrew Stock

Real-World Literacies: Disciplinary Teaching in the High School Classroom (2014) Heather Lattimer

Real-World Literacies

Disciplinary Teaching in the High School Classroom

Heather Lattimer
University of San Diego

National Council of Teachers of English
1111 W. Kenyon Road, Urbana, Illinois 61801-1096

Staff Editor: Bonny Graham

Series Editor: Cathy Fleischer

Interior Design: Victoria Pohlmann

Cover Design: Pat Mayer

Cover Photo: iStockphoto.com/sturti

NCTE Stock Number: 39431; eStock Number: 39448

ISBN 978-0-8141-3943-1; eISBN 987-0-8141-3944-8

It is the policy of NCTE in its journals and other publications to provide a forum for the open discussion of ideas concerning the content and the teaching of English and the language arts. Publicity accorded to any particular point of view does not imply endorsement by the Executive Committee, the Board of Directors, or the membership at large, except in announcements of policy, where such endorsement is clearly specified.

Every effort has been made to provide current URLs and email addresses, but because of the rapidly changing nature of the Web, some sites and addresses may no longer be accessible.

Library of Congress Cataloging-in-Publication Data

Lattimer, Heather, 1971–
    Real-world literacies : disciplinary teaching in the high school classroom / Heather Lattimer.
        pages cm
    Includes bibliographical references and index.
    ISBN 978-0-8141-3943-1 ((pbk))
    1. Language arts (Secondary) 2. Oral communication—Study and teaching (Secondary) 3. Thought and thinking—Study and teaching (Secondary) I. Title.
    LB1631.L265 2014
    428.0071'2—dc23
                                                    2014009792

For Andy, Matthew, and James.
You are my best teachers.
I am incredibly proud of each of you.

Contents

Acknowledgments

Teachers provided the inspiration for this book. Many, many thanks to the amazing educators who welcomed me into their classrooms and generously shared their expertise. Special thanks to Stacey Caillier, Aliza Cruz, Ben Daley, Jason Doherty, Jenni Doherty, Victoria Gichuhi, Cheryl Hibbeln, Gavin Ishihara-Wing, Steven Le, Charles Mbuto, Rob Meza-Ehlert, Caroline Mwangi, Diana Neebe, Rob Riordan, Jennifer Roberts, Alyssa Robledo, Larry Rosenstock, Mike Salamanca, Jena Workman, and Namir Yedid.

Much gratitude is owed to the teachers and early mentors who instilled in me a love for learning and a belief in the value of learning by doing. Special thanks to Larry Cuban, Hugh "Bud" Mehan, Wendy Porter, Liz Roselman, and Lee Swenson.

Thanks also to my university colleagues who provided support and encouragement, especially Viviana Alexandrowicz, Jerry Ammer, Donna Barnes, Sandy Buczynski, Paula Cordeiro, Linda Dews, Steve Gelb, Bobbi Hansen, Nancy Hanssen, Lea Hubbard, Nori Inoue, Helene Mandell, Michele McConnell, Maria Menezes, Sarina Molina, Reyes Quezada, George Reed, Sergio Rodriguez, Joi Spencer, Suzanne Stolz, and Mariam True. Appreciation also goes to my university students and alums for pushing my thinking, challenging me to clarify my explanations, and allowing me to travel with them on their educational journeys.

The editors and staff at NCTE have been patient, generous, and incredibly supportive. Special thanks to imprint editor Cathy Fleischer, who provided enthusiastic encouragement for this book every step of the way. Thanks also to Kurt Austin, Janet Brown, and Sharon Roth for their ongoing support; to reviewers whose feedback made the book stronger; and to the production team, especially Bonny Graham, Barbara Frazier, and Pat Mayer, for ensuring a beautiful final product.

Finally, and most important, thank you to family and friends. Thanks to my parents, "Grandma Carol and Bampa"; my children, Andy, Matthew, and James; and my wonderful husband, Joe, for putting up with my crazy hours and many procrastination techniques. Your love and support make everything possible.

Literacies *of* Disciplines

An NCTE Policy Research Brief

The Issue

Consider this: Fourth graders in the US score among the highest in the world on literacy assessments, but by tenth grade the same students score among the lowest. We know that the texts read by tenth graders are longer and more complex, demand greater abilities to synthesize information, and present conceptual challenges. All of these features are compounded by the fact that much of the reading done by tenth graders—actually all students beyond the fourth or fifth grade—is grounded in specific disciplines or content areas.[1]

The discrepancy between adolescent readers in the US and their peers elsewhere in the world and the apparent decline in literacy capacities as students move beyond elementary school suggests a problem that needs attention. A first step in addressing this issue is to examine the meanings carried by literacy and disciplines.

Literacies and Disciplines

Research over the past few decades shows that literacy is not a single or monolithic entity. Rather, it is a set of multi-faceted social practices that are shaped by contexts, participants, and technologies. This plurality is reflected in the many ways terms are taken up and used in research on literacy. For example, a survey of studies published in the *Journal of Literacy Research* found a wide range of meanings associated with the term *context*, which suggests that many related terms, including *literacy*, have multiple meanings. The plurality of literacy extends beyond the print-only world of reading and writing to new and developing technologies, along with visual, audio, gestural, spatial, or multimodal discourses. It is much more accurate, then, to adopt a perspective of plurality, to focus on literacies, recognizing the multiple values and meanings along with the ways literacies are inflected by different contexts.[2]

Disciplines is likewise a complicated term. One complication arises from the fact that disciplines, as they are conceived in higher education, do not exist in secondary schools. Content areas or school subjects in secondary schools are organized differently—social studies, for example, does not exist as a discipline although it is a high school subject—and school subjects often operate to constrain or control how knowledge is presented, while disciplines emphasize the creation of knowledge. Furthermore, while it is possible to identify general qualities—problem solving, empirical inquiry, research from sources, and performance—that distinguish academic areas from one another, the boundaries of disciplines are increasingly flexible and porous. No single discipline can function as a rigidly fixed container of knowledge. As Carter (2007) puts it, it is more productive to "emphasize not disjunction but junction, the intersections of disciplines, the connections between research and teaching, and the ties between writing and knowing. From this perspective, the issue is not so much writing in or outside but writing of the disciplines" (410).[3]

Literacies *of* Disciplines

Developing a New Model

Putting literacies next to disciplines adds another layer of complexity. Traditionally literacies and disciplines have come together as teachers have required students to utilize common strategies of reading and writing in each of their content-area classes. Research shows, however, that this approach does not engender student literacies in multiple disciplines. As Moje (2011) explains, "strategies—absent some level of knowledge, a purpose for engaging in the literate practice and an identification with the domain or the purpose—will not take readers or writers very far" (52). Instead, instruction is most successful when teachers engage their students in thinking, reading, writing, speaking, listening, and interacting in discipline-specific ways, where literacies and content are not seen as opposites but rather as mutually supportive and inextricably linked. When put next to literacies, then, disciplines represent unique languages and structures for thinking and acting; disciplines are spaces where students must encounter, be supported in, and be expected to demonstrate a plurality of literacies. This means taking a much more nuanced approach to disciplines and at the same time affirming the plurality of literacies. As such, all teachers play an equally important role because no one class or teacher can best develop students' literacies apart from discipline-informed resources and lenses.[4]

What Are the Benefits of Literacies of Disciplines?

Research shows that when schools create explicit spaces for students and teachers to discuss the overlap and the differences among disciplinary literacies, teachers become more effective, and students develop new ways of representing and generating knowledge. Learning in the discipline is fostered by multiple literacies, and the learning of literacies is likewise expanded. This process, in turn, enables students to traverse and to transfer learning across disciplines—thus enhancing their ability to become learners who make connections and draw distinctions to function more effectively, whether in classrooms or on-the-job.[5]

Classrooms where literacies of disciplines flourish are nurturing environments for formative assessment. The specificity of discipline-based literacies enables teachers and students to focus on only a few issues at a time, an essential feature for formative assessment because it allows teachers to give students the feedback they need to evaluate their own work without imposing grades. Teachers can use formative assessment to shape instruction based on student progress; considering student performance enables teachers to pinpoint areas where students may need more focused teaching. And teachers in specific disciplines are best prepared to assess student literacies in a given field. The processes associated with formative assessment help students relate new concepts to their prior knowledge in any discipline, making them more likely to transfer learning from one context to another.[6]

What Support Do Literacies of Disciplines Need?

Implementing literacies of disciplines will require significant attention to professional development for teachers. Teacher learning is an integral element not just of the teacher's continuing professional education, but also of student achievement. Teachers may learn in varying contexts—through their teaching experiences, school communities, conversations with colleagues, hallway interactions with students, or through professional development opportunities like workshops, inservices, or classes.

Regardless of how they learn, that learning will have a direct effect on what their students are able to accomplish. As the Common Core State Standards (CCSS) are implemented in most states across the nation, new forms of professional development will be required. The CCSS give literacies of disciplines a central position, and teachers will need professional development that addresses how the learning of literacies may be approached within their disciplines.

The professional development that will provide teachers with the resources and strategies necessary to support students in acquiring plural literacies needs to be sustained and systematic because episodic or unfocused learning experiences will not give teachers from multiple disciplines sufficient opportunities for effective learning. One of the most powerful forms of professional development is communities of practice. The National Writing Project exemplifies this approach by bringing together English language arts teachers from multiple schools for an intensive and sustained experience of learning, and research shows that this learning is transformative for teachers and their students. However, for literacies of discipline to flourish, a more cross-disciplinary form of professional development is needed.[7]

How Can We Develop Communities of Practice That Support Literacies of Disciplines?

By working with colleagues from several fields in the context of a long-term intentional community, teachers can become more aware of how their professional knowledge is developed through informal interactions. They can come to see their colleagues as resources for learning, and they can move smoothly between teaching and learning, implementing and reflecting on that implementation with colleagues. They can also gain deeper understandings of disciplinary literacy expectations by reading and discussing publications that address this issue. Experiences like these enable teachers to move beyond thinking of professional development as a one-time event and instead view it as an ongoing, recursive process that improves their own learning across different spaces and contexts. With this kind of professional development, teachers can support students as they learn to explore the multiple literacies of disciplines.[8]

Notes

1. UNESCO Institute for Statistics (2007). Global education digest: Comparing education statistics across the world. Montreal. Retrieved from http://www.uis.unesco.org/template/pdf/ged/2007/EN_web2.pdf

2. Russell, D. (2001). Where do the naturalistic studies point? A research review. In S. H. MacLeod, E. Miraglia, M. Soven, & C. Thaiss (Eds.), *WAC for the new millennium: Strategies for continuing writing-across-the-curriculum programs* (pp. 259–325). Urbana: NCTE.

Literacies *of* Disciplines

Rex, L., Green, J., Dixon, C., & Group, S. B. C. D. (1998). What counts when context counts?: The uncommon "common" language of literacy research. *Journal of Literacy Research, 30* (3), 405–433.

The New London Group (2000). "A pedagogy of multiliteracies: Designing social futures." In Bill Cope and Mary Kalantzis (Eds.), *Multiliteracies: Literacy learning and the design of social futures* (pp. 9–37). New York: Routledge.

3. Carter M. (2007). Ways of knowing, doing and writing in the disciplines. *College Composition and Communication, 58* (3), 385–418.

Heller, R. (2010). In praise of amateurism: A friendly critique of Moje's "call for change" in secondary literacy. *Journal of Adolescent & Adult Literacy, 54* (4), 267–273.

O'Brien, D. G., Steward, R. A., & Moje, E. B. (1995). Why content area literacy is difficult to infuse into the secondary school: Complexities of curriculum, pedagogy, and school culture. *Reading Research Quarterly, 30* (3), 442–463.

4. Draper, R. J., Broomhead, P., Jensen, A. P., Nokes, J. D., & Siebert, D. (Eds.). (2010). *(Re)imagining content-area literacy instruction.* New York: Teachers College Press & National Writing Project.

Langer, J. A. (2011). *Envisioning knowledge: Building literacy in the academic disciplines.* New York: Teachers College Press.

Moje, E. B. (2008). Responsive literacy teaching in secondary school content areas. In M. W. Conley, J. R. Freidhoff, M. B. Sherry, & S. F. Tuckey (Eds.), *Meeting the challenge of adolescent literacy: Research we have, research we need* (pp. 58–87). New York: Guilford Press.

Moje, E. B. (2008). Foregrounding the disciplines in secondary literacy teaching and learning: A call for change. *Journal of Adolescent & Adult Literacy, 52* (2), 96–107.

Moje, E. B. (2011). Developing disciplinary discourses, literacies and identities: What's knowledge got to do with it? In M. G. L. Bonilla and K. Englander (Eds.) *Discourses and identities in contexts of educational change: Contributions from the United States and Mexico* (49–74). New York: Peter Lang.

5. Bergman, L. S., & Zepernick, J. (2007). Disciplinary transfer: Students' perceptions of learning to write. *Writing Program Administration, 31* (1), 124–149.

Childers, P. B. (2007). High school-college collaborations: Making them work. *Across the Disciplines, 7.*

Graff, N. (2010). Teaching rhetorical analysis to promote transfer of learning. *Journal of Adolescent & Adult Literacy, 53* (5), 376–385.

Thaiss, C., & Zawacki, T. M. (2006). *Engaged writers dynamic disciplines: Research on the academic writing life.* Portsmouth: Heinemann.

Young, A. (2006). *Teaching writing across the curriculum.* Upper Saddle River, NJ: Pearson Prentice Hall.

6. Black, P., & Wiliam, D. (2009). Developing the theory of formative assessment. *Educational Assessment, Evaluation and Accountability, 21* (1), 5–31.

Cauley, K., & McMillan, J. (2010). Formative assessment techniques to support student motivation and achievement. *The Clearing House, 83* (1), 1–6.

Pryor, J., & Croussuard, B. (2008). A socio-cultural theorization of formative assessment. *Oxford Review of Education, 34* (1), 1–20.

7. Borko, H. (2004). Professional development and student learning: Mapping the terrain. *Educational Researcher, 33* (8), 3–15.

Whitney, A. (2008). Teacher transformation in the National Writing Project. *Research in the Teaching of English, 43* (2), 44.

8. Grossman, P., Wineburg, S., & Woolworth, S. (2001). Toward a theory of teacher community. *Teacher College Record, 103* (6), 942–1012.

Moje, E. B. (2008). Foregrounding the disciplines in secondary literacy teaching and learning: A call for change. *Journal of Adolescent and Adult Literacy, 52* (2), 92–107.

Webster-Wright, A. (2009). Reframing professional development through understanding authentic professional learning. *Review of Educational Research, 79* (2), 702.

This policy brief was produced by NCTE's James R. Squire Office of Policy Research, directed by Anne Ruggles Gere, with assistance from Elizabeth Homan, Will Hutchinson, Danielle Lillge, Justine Neiderhiser, Sarah Swofford, Crystal VanKooten, all students in the Joint PhD Program in English and Education at the University of Michigan, and Amanda Thompson, a student at the University of Virginia.

Literacy in the Imagination Age: Learning-by-Doing

I n his highly regarded TED Talks, education professor emeritus and thought leader Sir Ken Robinson offers a scathing critique of our current education systems, noting that too often we kill creativity and limit human capacity by failing to recognize and nurture a diversity of human talent. He argues that we need to fundamentally transform the structure of education in order to cultivate the talents of individual children as well as to be responsive to the rapidly changing demands of the twenty-first-century world.

> We have to change metaphors. We have to go from what is essentially an industrial model of education, a manufacturing model, which is based on linearity and conformity and batching people. We have to move to a model that is based more on principles of agriculture. We have to recognize that human flourishing is not a mechanical process; it is an organic process. You cannot predict the outcome of human development; all you can do is, like a farmer, create the conditions under which they will begin to flourish. (Robinson, 2010)

Comparative education scholar Yong Zhao (2009) arrives at a similar conclusion through his investigations of the American and the Chinese education models.

He finds irony in the fact that over the past decade, the United States has been working to standardize its education model, prioritizing rote skills and basic knowledge through standards, standardized testing, and adequate yearly progress (AYP) scores. This reform movement has been born largely out of fear that our position in the global economy is slipping, and slipping in particular to China. Meanwhile, in China, government leaders are looking to find ways to *de-standardize* the curriculum and cultivate more creativity through their education system. Chinese leaders recognize that to make the transition from being the "world's factory" to becoming a technology, innovation, and economy leader, schools need to do a better job of cultivating creative and diverse talents.

Observing the rapidly changing global economy and the emergence of new opportunities for communication, collaboration, and innovation provided through the creation of a virtual world, Zhao argues that we need to change our educational structures and goals:

> In the new era, we need more diverse talents rather than standardized laborers, more creative individuals rather than homogenized test takers, and more entrepreneurs rather than obedient employees. . . . To meet the challenges of the new era, American education needs to be more American, instead of more like education in other countries. The traditional strengths of American education—respect for individual talents and differences, a broad curriculum oriented to educating the whole child, and a decentralized system that embraces diversity—should be further expanded, not abandoned. (2009, pp. 181–82)

Robinson and Zhao join a chorus of voices arguing that in the beginning of the twenty-first century we are in the midst of a new transition from the information age to the "imagination age" (Pautler, 1998; Pucel, 1998). This era, they suggest, demands creativity, innovation, and imagination over analysis and evaluation. Because technology has democratized access to information, it is imagination—the ability to reconceptualize ideas, present information in new and creative ways, and develop innovative and original ways of thinking—that will add value to our economy and culture. Unfortunately, creativity and innovation, the very elements needed in the imagination age, are often devalued and diminished by our education systems. Quite frankly, despite the billions of dollars devoted to education by local municipalities, states, the federal government, and teachers like us who dedicate thousands of hours to help reform our system, the education we provide our students in too many cases does not meet the demands of the world they will encounter after they leave the K–12 system.

Why is this so? In part, it's because while the expectations for literacy have become increasingly complex, schools are too often stuck in a standardized, test-driven, knowledge-focused approach that fills our students' heads with information but often fails to ensure that they can critically respond to, critique, evaluate, and investigate that information or independently access new information that might complement or contradict the official knowledge presented in their textbooks.

Unpacking *Literacies* of *Disciplines*

NCTE's policy research brief *Literacies* of *Disciplines* (2011), reprinted on pages xi–xv, provides a pathway toward building teaching and learning practices that respond to the economic, professional, civic, community, and academic literacy demands of the twenty-first century. The policy brief defines *literacy* broadly, refer-ring, in fact, to *literacies* as a set of multifaceted social practices. Here, literacies are not defined as a particular text-based medium or a specific outcome but instead are seen as being adaptable to contexts, participants, and technologies. In other words, the term *literacies* encompasses communicating with friends and colleagues via text and email; searching and critically responding to information found online; creat-ing multimodal presentations that include charts, graphs, images, audio, and video; and participating in virtual and augmented reality simulations—as well as reading a novel or writing a paper. This definition of *literacies* recognizes that our notion of reading and writing is continually evolving in response to new contexts, new purposes, and new media. Developing competence in this new world of literacies requires more than phonemic awareness, the ability to decode and comprehend; it requires being able to recognize, adapt, and respond to new purposes, audiences, and forms—a definition that fits well with the demands of the twenty-first-century workplace, community, and civic life (Russell, 2001; Rex, Green, Dixon, & Santa Barbara Classroom Discourse Group, 1998; New London Group, 2000).

The policy brief similarly moves beyond our traditional school-bound defini-tion of disciplines. It emphasizes that *disciplines* are distinct from the *subjects* found in secondary schools. Whereas subjects are typically seen as silos or containers that hold and separate knowledge, NCTE's definition of *disciplines* emphasizes the cre-ation of knowledge and takes care to note that disciplinary boundaries are becom-ing increasingly porous (Carter, 2007; Heller, 2010; O'Brien, Stewart, & Moje, 1995). The distinction between subject and discipline is evident if you think about the varying roles of history as conceived in a high school classroom versus history as practiced by historians. Whereas high school history is often taught as "fixed and stable, dropped out of the sky readymade" (VanSledright, 2004, p. 232), those who work in the discipline of history are expected to revisit historical documents and interpretations with new questions to generate new learnings that have relevance to our understanding of both past and present. If we teach history from a disciplinary perspective, students are not expected to memorize information so much as they are expected to learn to question, read critically, suspend judgment, consider and effectively communicate new interpretations, and "cultivate puzzlement" (Wineburg, 2001)—a set of expectations that mirrors professional, academic, and civic demands of literacy in the twenty-first century.

What does this rethinking of the concepts of literacy and discipline mean for us as teachers? In many ways, it moves us beyond the popular notion of content area literacy as simply including some additional reading and writing assignments in science, math, and history classes. The policy brief challenges us to create spaces in which "students must encounter, be supported in, and be expected to demonstrate a plurality of literacies" (2; all page numbers cited are from the Web version). In other words, we must learn to recognize the unique languages and literacy structures that are represented by various disciplines and then help students both navigate within individual disciplines and travel among them (Bergmann & Zepernick, 2007; Childers, 2007; Graff, 2010; Thaiss & Zawacki, 2006; Young, 2006).

In his book *Time for Meaning*, literacy expert and former high school English teacher Randy Bomer describes his goals for teaching poetry: "I don't teach poetry so that kids will remember all about writing poems and be able to do it forever. I want them to develop habits of mind related to learning a genre, so that they can learn in whatever genres they need" (1995, p. 119). To meet the demands of *Literacies* of *Disciplines*, we must take a similar approach to disciplinary literacy. We must provide students with rich, inquiry-oriented learning experiences and teach them to learn how to learn. We must explicitly nurture habits of mind that will allow students to adapt literacy practices in response to evolving contexts, technologies, and disciplines. The literacy demands that students in our classrooms today will encounter in the workplace, academic sphere, and civic life in five, ten, or twenty years are nearly impossible to foresee. Framing teaching practices within robust definitions of both *literacies* and *disciplines*, and engaging students in learning experiences that authentically respond to these definitions, will allow them to succeed within disciplines today and prepare them to be successful as they traverse and transfer learning across disciplines and into new fields in the future.

Literacy Skills, the Imagination Age, and the Preparedness of Today's Graduates

So what will it take to prepare graduates of our K–12 schools to effectively navigate and lead in the imagination age? Our students will need literacy skills that empower them

- to read, understand, and critique new information and evolving ideas,
- to synthesize content across disciplines,
- to identify problems that need solving, and

- to develop new ideas and approaches and then explain, apply, and defend innovative thinking.

Proficiency in these areas requires mastery of basic literacy in reading, writing, listening, and speaking, but also the ability to go beyond the basics. No longer will it be enough to simply decode the words of a text and comprehend the meaning; graduates in the imagination age need to be able to

- analyze the material,
- critique its meaning,
- compare and connect across information sources, and
- apply the information or ideas presented to new situations and developing understandings.

And in their productive capacities, graduates must do more than restate and summarize. They need to use oral and written language

- to represent information in new and creative ways,
- to evaluate and respond to the ideas of others, and
- to effectively articulate and advocate for innovative ideas of their own.

So how are we doing? What do studies of recent high school graduates tell us about their readiness to effectively respond to the literacy demands of the imagination age?

Unfortunately, the news is fairly bleak. A number of measures indicate that as a nation we are proficient in neither basic literacy skills nor applied literacy practices. A 2006 workforce readiness survey of more than 400 employers from across the United States suggested that the majority of employers found high school graduates to be deficient in reading comprehension, writing in English, written communication, and critical thinking and problem solving (Casner-Lotto & Benner, 2006). A 2004 report on literacy in the workforce found that the nation's private employers spend an estimated $3.1 billion each year teaching their employees the literacy skills needed to be successful in their current positions (National Commission on Writing, 2004). Results from standardized tests reveal a similar pattern: the 2011 results for the National Assessment of Educational Progress (NAEP) writing test, often called the Nation's Report Card, found that only 24 percent of eighth- and twelfth-grade students tested as proficient in writing, while only 3 percent tested as advanced at each grade level.

If we segregate out results for those who plan to attend college, the news is not much better. The 2012 results of the SAT test showed reading scores at the lowest level since 1972 and writing scores down an average of nine points since 2006, when the writing section was introduced. Among 2012 high school graduates taking the ACT test, approximately two out of three met college readiness benchmarks in reading, while just over half met benchmarks in writing. College instructors estimate that 50 percent of high school graduates are prepared for college-level writing (Peter D. Hart Research Associates, Inc. & Public Opinion Strategies, 2005). As of 2004, almost 42 percent of all first-year students enrolled in public two-year colleges were enrolled in at least one remedial course (US Department of Education, National Center for Education Statistics, 2004).

Even for those of us who aren't swayed by data gathered through surveys and standardized tests, the portraits being drawn of classrooms around the country tell us we need to do more to prepare students for this new world. Although wonderful examples of innovative schools and classrooms doing incredible things certainly exist, many of us have witnessed, experienced, or been pressured to implement instruction that prioritizes skill drills and coverage over meaning making and innovation. We know that too many weeks of the school year are dedicated to test preparation and that too few opportunities are provided for in-depth learning, authentic questions, and creative problem solving.

Clearly, we need to do more. To prepare our graduates for the imagination age, schools must increase the quantity and transform the quality of literacy instruction. Reading, writing, listening, and speaking need to be taught across disciplines in ways that go beyond basic literacy skills to promote critical analysis, creative response, and innovative representation. Doing so will require that we reframe the conversation away from generalized strategy instruction and toward disciplinary literacy. Rather than focus on isolated reading, writing, and oral language skills, we must instead begin to consider how to engage students in using language to build understanding, effectively communicate in discipline-specific contexts, explore new ideas, and innovate in face-to-face and digital learning communities. And literacy instruction must be seamlessly integrated into content instruction so that it builds understanding in the disciplines and cultivates the four Cs of twenty-first-century skills: critical thinking, communication, collaboration, and creativity (Partnership for 21st Century Skills, 2011).

Moving toward an integrated literacy-as-grounded-learning requires a dramatic rethinking of our approach to instruction. It requires us to become designers of the learning experiences in our classrooms, recognizing external requirements, accessing community resources, and responding to the individual interests, strengths, and needs of our students. Rather than ceding control to textbook publishers, test developers, or perceived administrative demands, we need to take control of multiple competing demands on classroom time and content instruction to create learning opportunities that cultivate content understanding, literacy skills, and critical thinking, creativity, and innovation.

Initially, this approach may seem overwhelming, particularly if we view it through the prism of isolated skill and content instruction that, sadly, has become the norm in our era of standardized testing. However, as the following examples demonstrate, if we step back to consider how to build on what we already know about best practice instruction, we can find opportunities to create meaningful learning experiences that concurrently nurture content understanding, literacy skill development, and twenty-first-century skills.

Literacies of the Disciplines in Action

The following two examples come from secondary schools I've had the opportunity to work with in Southern California. Both courses focus on science learning and both make efforts to integrate literacy into the science content. Both, in other words, focus on helping students attain certain kinds of disciplinary literacies. You'll see immediately, however, that their approaches are very different and consequently so are the results. As you read, ask yourself how the instruction and the learning in these classrooms differ, how the students are positioned as learners, and how the teachers position themselves.

Unit on the Immune System

Colleen Wilson teaches tenth-grade biology at Ocean View High,[1] a large comprehensive school located in a working-class community on the edge of a large city. In mid-March, Colleen's biology classes begin a unit on the immune system. It is one of Colleen's favorite units because the course material provides so many practical connections. She launches the unit with several teacher-selected human interest stories intended to pique students' interest and YouTube videos that include graphic images of disease symptoms.

Students then read the relevant chapters from their textbooks, using a Cornell note-taking structure to assist in reading comprehension. Because the unit takes place in the second semester, students are already familiar with the structure of Cornell notes (see Figure 1.1) and how to use headings and other text features to develop reading comprehension questions and identify relevant information in the text. Most are able to complete the reading on their own and do well on the reading quiz used to assess their content knowledge.

Conscious of the need for greater student engagement to ensure content retention as well as the potential for making connections to students' lives outside of class, Colleen supplements the textbook with a simulation activity and several news articles about recent outbreaks of diseases. The simulation consists of students demonstrating the exponential rate of the spread of disease by distributing brightly

Figure 1.1. Sample Cornell notes.

Name: Date: Period:

Key Points	Details

The Human Immune System

1.) There are 3 Lines of Defense

① Barriers - Skin
                - mucous membranes
                - Cilia
                - Stomach acid

② Inflammatory response
    - more blood flow
    - higher body temp
    Phagocytes ingest microbes
    Interferons block cell-to-cell
                                infection

③ Adaptive immunity
    T-cells
    B lymphocytes

2.) 3 phases of immune response

① Recognition
② Activation
③ Effector

Summary

The body has many ways to protect against disease. Skin and mucus membranes provide barriers. Inflamation can make it hard for viruses and bacteria to survive. Lymphocytes can make antibodies that ~~still~~ provide immunity.

Freeology.com   Free School Stuff

colored stickers among their classmates. Students read the news articles about outbreaks of the flu, Ebola, and tuberculosis independently and then discuss them with their peers. Students also respond to each of these articles through a written response in the journals they keep for science class.

The culminating activity of the unit is an independent research project. This project provides an opportunity for students to strengthen their understanding of the science content and also supports the tenth-grade faculty goal of engaging students in at least three research projects in different disciplines during the course of the school year. Students are randomly assigned a focus disease and provided with a series of guiding questions. Colleen leads students through the research process—teaching them how to use note cards to record information, providing an organizational guide for the structure of the paper, demonstrating appropriate citation of sources, and modeling the proper use of scientific language. At the end of the unit, each student turns in a five-page, double-spaced paper that is scored against a research rubric. If the paper scores well, it may be included in the student's academic portfolio.

Reading through students' reports, Colleen is generally pleased with the students' work. Most of them completed and submitted their work on time or close to it, they demonstrated core knowledge of the topic, and many have shown growth in their research and writing skills. But sitting down to grade the reports on a Saturday night after everyone else in her family has gone to bed, Colleen finds herself contemplating why she seems to work so much harder than her students do and wondering if the students care as much about their learning as she does.

Community Health Project

Just a few miles away from Colleen's classroom, Janie Campbell, a tenth-grade biology teacher at Innovations Academy, is preparing to launch a community health project. After the class settles in, Janie introduces Mercedes Rodriguez, the lead nurse practitioner at the local health clinic. Dressed in a white lab coat and still wearing a stethoscope around her neck, Nurse Rodriguez begins by sharing statistics on the incidence of disease in the local community. She notes that this neighborhood, which includes working-class residents, a large immigrant community, and off-base military housing, has significantly greater health concerns than those of surrounding neighborhoods. "We offer many services at the clinic," she explains, "but typically, by the time we see patients they are already sick. What we need is more education to inform the community about disease risks and prevention strategies. You are members of this community and we need your leadership to create a media campaign."

Nurse Rodriguez and Janie then tag-team to provide an overview of the assignment: Students will create a series of educational videos about diseases that pose the greatest risk to the community. Videos that meet standards in accuracy and quality will be posted to YouTube and the clinic's website, run on a continuous loop on screens in the clinic's lobby and the neighborhood library, and broadcast on local TV stations.

Although initially a bit intimidated by the scope and import of the task, Janie's students soon take ownership of the project. At Janie's suggestion, they have conversations with friends and family members, which reveal some of the human stories behind the statistics that Nurse Rodriguez presented. These stories help students realize that disease prevention is a real and immediate need they can do something about.

With Janie's guidance, students develop a list of the things they will need to know to create informative and engaging videos and then set about their research. They begin by using their textbooks to develop general background knowledge about cell biology, disease, and immunity. They then split into teams to learn details about their focus diseases, including hepatitis C, influenza, pertussis, strep, and tuberculosis. For this research, students rely heavily on medical reference texts, skimming and scanning to find the relevant sections and then reading those materials closely to ensure accurate understanding. When more nuanced questions demand more detailed answers, students, with scaffolding support from Janie and the school librarian, dig into scientific journal articles and online databases available from a nearby university library. In addition, Janie invites local physicians, a biology professor, and a public health official into the classroom to provide up-to-date information on the latest disease treatment and prevention practices and to answer student-generated questions.

As students conclude their initial research phase, they start to craft storyboard outlines for their videos. They work in teams to synthesize information into a coherent educational message; create an engaging hook; develop a compelling narrative; create visuals that would inform and engross; and select facts, statistics, and anecdotes that effectively communicate their message. Along the way, they hold teacher conferences and peer critique sessions during which they are continuously challenged to transform the information they have learned from their research into a product specifically tailored for their community audience. As they work, students return again and again to their research materials—double (or triple) checking their facts, seeking out new details to help communicate a particular point, and working to make sure that what they are creating is accurate and relevant. "This is going to be seen by people from our community," one student comments. "It could be my cousins or my neighbors who watch it. It has to be good and it has to be right. If not, I will be letting them down by not providing them with the information they need to stay healthy."

As students plan, film, and edit their videos, they reach out to experts in the field and to other teachers who are part of the tenth-grade team. Nurse Rodriguez visits the classroom on several occasions, checking in on students' progress and offering suggestions informed by her firsthand knowledge of the target audience. Students send drafts of their videos to an epidemiologist at a nearby medical school who gives feedback on the accuracy of their facts and the integrity of the presentation. Students consult with their math teacher, Philip King, to get help with data graphing and statistical representation, prevail upon English teacher Connie Nash to critique their video scripts, and get instruction in video editing, voice-over, and the art of digital animation from media instructor Will Evans.

In the days leading up to students' video presentations, students scramble to conduct final fact checks, finish editing their animations, and polish their presentation techniques. When the big day arrives, students come to school dressed in their best "professional" attire. Although Janie notices their nerves (and acknowledges she has quite a few butterflies herself), when the students step up to the podium to present their work to panels of health care professionals, media experts, educators, and community members, they appear poised and knowledgeable.

One at a time, teams share their videos, explain their objectives, describe their learning, answer panelists' questions, and reflect on the process. "I learned a lot about myself," one student tells the panel. "I learned how to set deadlines, do research, work with the other people in my group, and take responsibility to do my best." Another student reflects, "I didn't think I was going to like this project because it seemed like a lot of work and I didn't know anything about hepatitis when we first started. But I feel really proud now that we are done. I learned a lot about disease and feel much more knowledgeable about biology and medicine now. And the video we made is good. I showed it to my little brother last night and he thought so too. I like that we made something that can help other people."

After the final presentation, Janie congratulates her students and then collapses into a chair. The previous weeks have been exhausting but immensely satisfying. "I'm so proud of my kids," Janie exudes. "They worked incredibly hard on this project and really took ownership over their work." Her pride is well founded. Feedback from the panelists who attended the presentations is overwhelmingly positive. Comments include the following: "Fantastic work! You knew the content and were able to make it accessible and relevant for your audience. Well done!"; "I was so impressed by your knowledge and professionalism. I hope you consider careers in the health sciences"; and "I was stunned by the depth of your understanding. You were quoting from sources I didn't begin to read until my junior and senior year of college. Very impressive!"

Janie would be the first to acknowledge that there were bumps along the way as the community health project progressed: some students struggled to find accessible reading materials, several teams had difficulty coming to an agreement around their video storyboard, and a few students stumbled during their presentations. But overall the project did for students what Janie wanted it to do: it built deep content understanding. As the principal commented to me after the students' presentations, "These kids really know their stuff. And not just the stuff about diseases. They are beginning to talk like scientists, think like scientists, and think of themselves as scientists. This was a powerful learning experience."

A Tale of Two Units

These two units, the immune system unit at Ocean View High and the community health project at Innovations Academy, were taught to similar populations of students and had similar content learning objectives. Both addressed core competencies in the high school biology curriculum. Both included activities designed to engage students in the material. Both worked to integrate literacy standards into the curriculum. However, the learning experience for students in the two classrooms was very different. A central point of difference concerns the concept of real-world learning and authentic literacy. While Colleen's unit on the immune system at Ocean View High did a good job of creating a school-based learning experience, the community health project at Innovations Academy connected science content and literacy development to expectations and understandings demanded in the world outside of school.

So what were the underlying differences in these classrooms? As I observed the two units, I was struck by five key points of comparison that distinguished these approaches to disciplinary learning:

• **Authentic purpose and audience.** The community health project was grounded in a real need in the community. Students were invited to participate in doing real work for a real client for distribution to a real audience. Knowing that their work was going to be viewed by individuals from their local community increased students' motivation to ensure accuracy in the content and quality of their product. This approach reflects the reality of life after high school: you may not always get to choose your purpose or the audience for your work, but there is always a purpose and an audience that matters. Learning how to adapt to that purpose and respond to the interests and needs of the audience is essential for success.

By contrast, the unit on the immune system included products, such as a research paper and Cornell notes, whose purpose was limited to the classroom and an audience limited to the teacher. Although the knowledge and skills gained from such activities have the potential for wider applicability, if students do not learn how to adapt to varying purposes and audiences through guided learning experiences while in school, we are limiting their understanding and ability to do so after they leave us. Engaging students in content and literacy learning with authentic purposes and audiences increases students' motivation, deepens their content knowledge, and prepares them with both the skills and the ability to adapt those skills to specific contexts in their future academic and professional interactions.

• **Flexible processes and negotiable structures.** Both units engaged students in structured learning experiences. Both required students to read texts and to write documents. However, the approaches to this learning varied greatly. The unit on the immune system taught reading and writing through a linear approach. Students were instructed to use a research methodology that progressed step by step from information gathering to outlining to drafting to editing to completion. They were required to read the relevant textbook chapters from start to finish, taking notes on all of the information the publishers had identified as important through the use of headings, key terms, and other text features. Students were provided with a generic outline that structured their research paper for them, giving them both physical and metaphorical boxes in which to group their information and ideas. Each of these structures was intended to help scaffold the learning for students, providing them with supports to break down complex literacy activities and make them accessible for novice readers and writers in the discipline. The drawback, however, is that this linear approach bears little resemblance to the processes and structures students will encounter in the world outside of school.

In contrast, students participating in the community health project engaged in more iterative processes that more closely approximate literacy activities in the real world. Textbooks and other reference materials were not read from start to finish but instead approached as resources that could be skimmed and scanned to locate the content relevant to the questions that arose in the research process. The research process did not proceed in neat and isolated steps with clear boundaries between asking questions, information gathering, outlining, etc. Instead, Janie recognized that new information often leads to new questions and that organizing material into a work product for an audience often reveals holes in the data or the need for new resources. During the research process, students in the community health project were encouraged to move back and forth between research phases in response to the questions and needs that arose; most came to recognize that research is never "done" but is an ongoing quest for new learning so that we can better understand concepts and more powerfully represent information and ideas. Similarly, the writing that occurred in storyboarding and scriptwriting for the videos, while grounded in familiar narrative and persuasive text structures, needed to cross genre boundaries and adapt to the content and purpose of the project. The literacy activities in Janie's classroom had their foundations in established reading, writing, and research processes and structures but then encouraged students to go beyond them. Students were encouraged and provided with support to adapt their literacy work to the needs of the project. This is an approach that is much more reflective of and better preparation for the ways in which they will use literacy in the real world.

• **Teacher as facilitator.** When schools connect students with purposes and audiences outside of school, the dynamic of the teacher–student relationship changes. In the traditional classroom, such as that demonstrated by the immune system unit, the teacher's role is to establish priorities, determine content, deliver instruction, and evaluate student learning. The power and the opportunity to do the "thinking work" in the classroom rest almost entirely with the teacher. Colleen identified the texts that would be read, the questions that would be asked, the topics that would be researched, and the research paper structures that would be used. To an extent, this is entirely appropriate; teachers are expected to be more knowledgeable about both content and content literacy than their students in order to take a lead role in establishing expectations. But when the balance of decision making rests so heavily with the teacher, it removes opportunities for students to think critically about content. Further, it represents a level of micromanagement that, in the working world, would likely be frustrating for both employer and employee.

A teacher–student relationship that is much more responsive to the dynamic working relationship seen in most industries today is present in the community health project classroom. Here, Janie worked with students to set expectations and establish guidelines that were responsive to the project's purpose and audience. She provided content background to shape context for their project and guided them toward topic-appropriate resources. She taught literacy strategies and research processes but then allowed students flexibility to adapt the materials and strategies to fit the content and objectives of their individual work products. She checked in regularly, working with students individually and in small groups to assess content understanding, provide feedback, make suggestions, and redirect where necessary. This guided approach gave students the freedom to try things out, develop new approaches, and be creative. It demanded that students think critically about the content, asking questions, evaluating sources, and identifying strengths and weaknesses in their own work. And, because the work was iterative, with multiple assessment points along the way, the guided approach provided opportunities for students to make mistakes, assess their failings, reflect on their learning, and, with the support of their teacher and their peers, revise their work and strengthen their understanding. This type of facilitated learning encourages students to become independent, proactive, and responsive in their approach to problem solving, qualities that surveys of employers consistently stress as priorities for the workforce of the twenty-first century.

• **Access to experts.** Both Colleen and Janie care deeply about their disciplines and want to ensure that students recognize the relevance and importance of the topics being studied. However, their approaches to meeting this objective varied significantly. Janie brought content experts into the classroom. She introduced her students to health care professionals and biomedical scientists who provided students with targeted mentoring for the community health project. She asked experts in the discipline to give students feedback during the process and then to sit on the panels that assess the final videos and presentations. She required students to find, read, and evaluate texts that are authentic to the discipline. And she encouraged her students to reach out to other teachers on campus, who brought their specialized knowledge of statistical representation and animation to support students' work.

In contrast, Colleen took on herself the responsibility for providing expertise. She selected the texts that students read, answered their questions, and read and graded all of their papers. Some might argue that this is what a teacher should do. After all, we are hired in part based on our content knowledge. But when we take all of that responsibility on ourselves, we limit our students' opportunity to develop deep understanding of the discipline. The reason for this is two-fold: (1) No matter how dedicated a learner you are, it is unlikely that you or any teacher will be able to stay fully abreast of scholars' evolving understanding across all the topics of your discipline. Connecting to the latest literature and to professionals who are dedicated experts on a particular topic gives students access to a much greater depth of understanding. (2) Outside of high school, learning opportunities won't be predesigned for students. They will need to understand how to connect to resources, both in person and in text, that can contribute to their learning. They will need to know how to seek out experts, ask thoughtful questions, sort through conflicting responses, and connect the information to knowledge they already have. Helping students to develop these practices while still in school prepares them with the knowledge, skills, and dispositions necessary to connect with experts in the real world.

• **Student ownership.** In both of the units profiled here, students did a significant amount of work either on their own or with their peers. However, only in the community health project did students truly own the work they completed. The authenticity of the project and the dynamic of teacher-as-facilitator allowed students to take ownership of both the product and the process through which they worked—to become agents in their own learning. They made choices about what was created and how it was made. As in the real world, the choices were circumscribed by the needs of the client, the availability of resources, and the expectations of their leader, in this case teacher Janie Campbell. However, the available options gave students the latitude to create a product that they determined was most appropriate to their purpose and best suited to their audience. They owned the results and, for better or for worse, had to take responsibility for the work they created.

Student ownership was less evident in the immune system unit. Colleen made many of the choices for students. Reading and research topics were assigned; the report structure was predetermined. Furthermore, the lack of an authentic audience meant that students had less of an incentive to create something that was truly unique and meaningful since it would be read by only one person before being assigned a grade and filed away.

As I observed in both classes, the enthusiasm gap was palpable. Students at Ocean View were completing the activities in the immune system unit, but most were doing the work because they felt obligated to, not because they truly wanted to. On the other hand, nearly all of the Innovations Academy students expressed significant enthusiasm for and pride in their work. Students who had previously been labeled as underperforming stepped up and worked hard on the project. At the culminating panel presentations, students were able to describe in detail the choices they had made, the thinking behind their choices, and their assessment of the quality of their work. They reflected on their own learning and identified areas of strength and areas for growth.

This sense of responsibility, reflectiveness, and pride of ownership is necessary for life outside of high school, where grades are not assigned, standardized tests don't determine job or career prospects, and success is determined by a willingness to work hard, take ownership, and engage as a learner, always seeking to improve. By providing students with opportunities to own their work while in school, we empower them with agency. Although they are novices, high school students can make real contributions to disciplinary conversations. Engaging our students in work that requires them to take responsibility for their learning not only provides them with the dispositions and knowledge to contribute in the future, but it also positions them to have a voice in shaping the field right now, valuing both their future potentials and their present strengths.

What Can We Learn from These Two Units?

Even if you're convinced that these five curricular concepts—authentic purpose and audience, flexible processes and negotiable structures, teacher as facilitator, access to experts, and student ownership—hold promise for student success, you still may find the reach of the work in the Innovations Academy classroom a bit daunting. The level of cooperation among teachers, the flexibility in curricular approaches, and the responses of the students may seem like a dream come true! My observations in these and other settings, though, have shown me that such work is indeed possible. While it's true that Janie Campbell received a great deal of support from administration and colleagues, at the heart of this classroom is a commitment to a different kind of education, one that is situated in a conception of *learning-by-doing*. With this goal at the center of disciplinary and literacy instruction, all kinds of educational possibilities open up. In subsequent chapters, you'll get the chance to see history teachers, literature teachers, science teachers, and math teachers open up their classrooms to real-world literacy grounded in this conception, all with different approaches situated in their own contexts.

Grounding Real-World Literacy in Theory and Research

The community health project at Innovations Academy integrates twenty-first-century skills and up-to-date media tools to shape disciplinary literacy into learning experiences with real-world relevance. However, the foundations of this unit and other similarly oriented classroom experiences are certainly not new to the twenty-first century. John Dewey, father of the progressive movement in American education in the late nineteenth and early twentieth centuries, advocated for a school curriculum that engages students in "learning by doing" (Dewey, 1916). More recent instructional reform movements that incorporate a learning-by-doing approach include inquiry education, project-based learning, and linked learning.

> • *Inquiry Education.* An inquiry approach to education begins with open-ended questions. Students learn by responding to these questions through reading, research, discussion, and problem solving, facilitated and supported by their teachers. Inquiry education builds on the work of cognition research by Bruner (1966), Piaget (1971), and Vygotsky (1962), who argued against the transmission approach to education that was the norm at the time, typified by lecture and rote memorization. They posited instead that learning occurs through active student engagement with new ideas and information in a manner that allows the construction of individual and community understanding. More recent contributors to inquiry learning include Banchi and Bell's (2008) work on levels of

Classroom Application

Consider how these five concepts apply in your own classroom. What are you already doing? How could you strengthen these practices in the future?

- **Authentic purpose and audience**—Are students responding to real needs and questions? Will students share their work with an audience of peers, mentors, or community members?

- **Flexible processes and negotiated structures**—Do students have opportunities to revisit information and ideas as they learn more? Are students encouraged to ask and explore questions?

- **Teacher as facilitator**—Are students given responsibility for problem solving with guidance and support from the teacher? Are mistakes seen as opportunities for learning?

- **Access to experts**—Do students have opportunities to interact with experts in the field under investigation? Are experts providing mentorship to students as they build their own disciplinary understanding?

- **Student ownership**—Are there opportunities for student choice? Do students take pride in their work? Do students have agency to determine their success?

inquiry-based instruction in science; Beach and Myers's (2001) discussion of inquiry-based literature learning in English; and Carpenter, Fennema, Franke, Levi, and Empson's work on cognitively guided instruction in mathematics (1999).

• *Project-Based Learning.* In project-based learning (PBL), students are challenged to design a project such as a physical model, visual presentation, or digital representation that demonstrates their understanding of the subject under investigation and presents an original response to an authentic audience. Unlike what we might think of as more traditional school projects, such as the diorama book project or sugar cube pyramid, that typically come at the end of a unit and are intended to demonstrate what has been learned, PBL takes the stance that the project drives the learning, encouraging students to investigate and uncover core concepts in order to respond to the challenges posed by the project demands (Lattimer & Riordan, 2011; Markham, Larmer, & Ravitz, 2003). Research into the results of PBL suggests that it has a positive impact on students' motivation and engagement (Yetkiner, Anderoglu, & Capraro, 2008) and that it can be more effective than traditional instruction in supporting concept mastery, long-term knowledge retention, and critical thinking and analysis skills (see, e.g., Boaler, 1997; Strobel & van Barneveld, 2009; Walker & Leary, 2009).

• *Linked Learning.* Started in response to concerns about tracking, linked learning is a whole-school model that insists that all students, regardless of background or previous achievement, need to be prepared for success in college, career, and community life. Schools organized in a linked learning approach engage students in learning experiences that are both equitable and individualized through themed academies, internships, community service learning, and project-based learning that promote academic, professional, and civic achievement. Although a relatively young movement, linked learning has already produced significant evidence demonstrating that such an approach can have a positive impact on closing the achievement gap and raising overall performance (Center for Advanced Research and Technology, 2011; Hoachlander, Stearns, & Studier, 2008).

About This Book

The inspiration for this book comes from my own classroom teaching experience as well as my work with teachers in schools. I started my teaching career twenty years ago as a high school social studies teacher at Lincoln High School in San Jose. Assigned to the most challenging group of ninth-grade students, I tried everything I could think of to get students to engage, but not much seemed to work. Then one day I challenged students to research, write, and present the his-

tory of their communities. Despite some initial complaints and lots of foot drag-
ging, nearly everyone did the work, they learned more twentieth-century history
than I could have imagined, and they dressed in their Sunday best to present their
findings to parents, school officials, and community leaders. The students were so
proud of themselves, and I was immediately hooked on the idea of making learning
authentic.

Today, as a university-based teacher educator, I continue to advocate for
a learning-by-doing approach, and whenever possible I immerse myself in classrooms that are grounded in a similar philosophy. The examples in the pages that
follow are drawn from these classrooms. In the San Diego area, where I now work,
we are fortunate to have some incredible schools and teachers who have adopted
school-wide learning-by-doing models using project-based learning or linked
learning approaches. And we have amazing educators who "teach in the cracks"
(Short, Schroeder, Kauffman, & Kaser, 2005), carving out space within more traditionally structured institutions to create innovative learning environments that are
responsive to student needs.

Each time I visit these schools and classrooms, I come away inspired. I'm
excited to be able to share some of their work in this book.

A preview of what is to come: Chapters 2 through 4 explore reading, writing, listening, and speaking and how these elements of literacy play out across the
disciplines in a variety of classrooms where teachers are working hard to create
a learning-by-doing approach. Chapter 5 addresses how teachers committed to
these processes think about reflection, peer critique, and the ever-present assessment. The postscript provides practical tips for moving toward implementation
while navigating the very real obstacles that we encounter as teachers in real-world
classrooms. Each of these chapters provides clear guidelines and offers descriptive
classroom portraits of teachers and students at work. Additionally, each connects
the discussion to current findings of student achievement and research around best
practices in the literacies of the disciplines.

I hope that as you read you dive into the ideas explored in each chapter,
consider how they might connect to your classroom and your students, try out
implementation in the classroom, and then assess the impact on student learning.
And as you go, I encourage you to discuss your findings with colleagues and reflect
on the implications for your teaching practice. I can't stress enough that these
classroom portraits are meant as examples of what has worked for particular teachers in particular settings. These teachers would be the first to tell you that the ideas
are meant to be adaptable to your own setting. One of the core principles of real-
world and discipline-based literacy is that teaching and learning must be authentic,
responsive, and context driven. Taking an idea and adapting it to the interests of

your students, the demands of your school, and the needs of your community isn't "cheating"; it is responding to the world around you and modeling the critical approaches and real-world practices we want to encourage for our students.

A Final Note

Although much of the conversation about applied learning and real-world literacy connects this work with better preparation for student success in college, work, and professional life, it is important to note that many of the advocates for these approaches to teaching and learning ground their advocacy in the goal of creating a better society. Dewey, for example, wrote extensively about the link between education and democracy, claiming that for democracy to thrive, meaningful and authentic educational experiences must be the norm for all children:

> Democracy cannot flourish where the chief influences in selecting subject matter of instruction are utilitarian ends narrowly conceived for the masses. . . . The notion that the "essentials" of elementary education are the three R's mechanically treated, is based upon ignorance of the essentials needed for the democratic ideas. Unconsciously it assumes that these ideals are unrecognizable; it assumes that in the future, as in the past, getting a livelihood, "making a living," must dignify for most men and women doing things which are not significant, freely chosen, and ennobling to those who do them. (1916, p. 200)

Inquiry education advocates Neil Postman and Charles Weingartner argue in *Teaching as a Subversive Activity* (1971) that teaching students to engage in asking and responding to authentic questions both prepares them to succeed in the world as it exists and positions them with the skills and understanding needed to promote change toward a more democratic and egalitarian society. "Once you have learned how to ask questions—relevant and appropriate and substantial questions—you have learned how to learn and no one can keep you from learning whatever you want or need to know" (p. 23).

More recently, in the 1990s and 2000s, PBL and linked learning advocates including Deborah Meier, Ted Sizer, the George Lucas Educational Foundation, and the Coalition of Essential Schools have all advocated for educational approaches in classrooms, schools, and school systems that enhance equality and opportunity in education. The first common principle of the Coalition for Essential Schools is "learning to use one's mind well," with a vision that schools should equip "all students with the intellectual, emotional, and social habits and skills to become powerful and informed citizens who contribute actively toward a democratic and equitable society" (CES, n.d.). Ted Sizer, former dean of the Harvard Graduate School of Education and cofounder of the Coalition of Essential Schools, writes of the transformative power of school:

School exists to change young people. The young people should be different—better—for their experience there. They should know some important things, they should know how to learn additional important things, and they should be in the habit of wanting to learn such important things. They should have a reasoned, but individual point of view. They should be judicious, aware of the complexity of the world. They should be thoughtful, respectful of thought and of ideas which are the furniture of thought. (Sizer & Sizer, 2000, p. 103)

Engaging students in real-world literacy is crucial if we are to nurture the development of the judicious, thoughtful, and respectful young people Sizer envisions. Grappling with authentic questions and meaningful literacy experiences while in school will prepare students for individual success in college and career while also preparing them to improve our collective success as a community, nation, and world. This approach to teaching is challenging in many ways. It confronts the current standardized testing paradigm and demands that teachers take ownership of designing the learning experiences in their classrooms. It requires us to be more knowledgeable about our students and more responsive to individual interests and community needs. It is tough work. And it is essential if we are to truly educate for the twenty-first century.

**Chapter
Two**

Reading for Learning

Hector Sanchez always knew he wanted to work with cars. What he didn't anticipate when he became a mechanic nearly three decades ago was how much cars would change. The complicated computer-based systems of today's automobiles require that he stay up-to-date with rapidly evolving technology. To do so, he must be able to read, interpret, understand, and apply multiple sets of online schematics and digital manuals. To ensure that Hector and his colleagues can meet the demands of high-tech auto repair, the national auto repair chain where they work requires that all mechanics regularly review manufacturer updates and pass monthly online examinations.

Lucy Nguyen works as a human resources manager at a large multinational corporation. Assigned to support the research and development division, Lucy must be able to read and respond to a wide range of texts every day, including performance evaluations, emails, job applicant résumés, and continuously updated HR policies that respond to new state, federal, and international regulations. Staying on top of a broad range of information allows Lucy to effectively advise executives about hiring, firing, managing, and supporting personnel within the division.

Sara Gould is a registered nurse by training and a stay-at-home mom to three young children. Her daily reading includes a healthy diet of picture books read aloud to her youngest children and second-grade homework sheets that she figures out with her older son. Additionally, she encounters communications from both the elementary school and the preschool, some with important dates and others filled with legal jargon, and a collection of bills, warranties, insurance forms, and bank and credit card statements that help her keep the household running. In her few moments of downtime, Sara tries to keep up with developments in the health care field. She plans to renew her nursing license and return to work when her youngest child starts kindergarten.

Craig Dodd runs a small organic farm on land inherited from his grandparents. An early adopter in the move toward organic farming, Craig has spent significant time online over the past decade researching everything from irrigation and fertilizer techniques to pest control remedies, weather predictions, and marketing strategies. In addition, Craig serves as an elected representative with the local agricultural board, a position that requires him to read and assess lengthy regulation proposals and resource management plans for monthly board meetings.

The Need for Reading Competence

As the examples of Hector, Lucy, Sara, and Craig demonstrate, the demand for reading proficiency has increased in nearly all sectors of our society. Technology has changed the way we live and work, evolving the kinds of jobs we do and the literacy demands within those jobs (Biancarosa & Snow, 2006), as well as the kinds of reading competencies we need for civic, community, and family life. No longer is it enough to be trained in a profession before entering the labor market; it is now essential that workers and citizens continually update their knowledge and hone their skills. To do so, critical reading skills are crucial. Nearly everyone, from highly educated professionals to service industry workers to blue-collar employees to ordinary citizens and parents, needs to be able to access information, read and comprehend that information, critically evaluate sources, and determine relevance and applicability.

A 2006 survey of more than 400 employers found that reading comprehension ranked at or near the top of the list of "very important" skills for job success in the workforce among entrants at all education levels—high school graduates, two-year college graduates, and four-year college graduates (Casner-Lotto & Benner, 2006). Reading was consistently viewed as more critical than knowledge and skills in math, science, foreign languages, and economics. Understanding this demand requires that we rethink what we mean by *reading*: professionals such as Sara Gould must be able to access and evaluate new scientific knowledge, managers such as Lucy Nguyen have to read and accurately apply evolving company policies, laborers such as Hector Sanchez must stay up-to-date on technical demands of the machines with which they are working, and self-employed small business owners like Craig Dodd have to be able to read, navigate, and critically analyze a wide range of information, technical data, and advice.

Keeping up with evolving technology, new policies, and new learning requires both critical reading skills and the ability to access and understand increasingly complex and varied forms of text. A 2010 report by the Council of Chief State School Officers and the National Governors Association Center on Best Practices found that the complexity of workplace materials has significantly increased over the past fifty years (CCSSO & NGA, 2010). Another survey, conducted in 2000, found that 38 percent of job applicants taking employer-administered tests lacked the reading skills needed in the jobs for which they had applied, a percentage that had doubled in just four years for the same jobs, demonstrating the rapid pace of increase in the expectations for reading proficiency in the workforce (Center for Workforce Preparation, 2002).

Beyond the workplace, demands have increased as well. College courses, for example, have always been text heavy, and with the advent of online and hybrid course options, increasing amounts of independent reading and learning are expected of university students. Studies in higher education have found that reading competence is often a prerequisite for enrolling in academically challenging courses (Au, 2000) and is nearly always a requirement for mastering content in science as well as humanities-based disciplines (Joftus, 2002). Similarly, in civic, community, and family life, reading is a necessity for full participation and engagement as a voter, community member, consumer, and parent. For example, to be an effective representative, Craig Dodd needs to be able to read and critically analyze regulation proposals that come before the county agricultural board; and as a mom, Sara Gould needs to read and respond to school forms, billing statements, and insurance policies to look out for the best interests of her children. Knowing and understanding rights and responsibilities and being able to make informed decisions requires that individuals be able to read notices, research information, maintain an awareness of current events, critically evaluate sources, and apply learning. And as anyone who has recently read a ballot initiative or bank statement can attest, the materials we are presented with are increasingly complex. To survive in the twenty-first-century world, reading competence and confidence is essential.

Reading Achievement: What Our High School Graduates Can Do

Unfortunately, an abundance of evidence suggests that too many of our high school graduates are not prepared with the necessary reading competence and confidence. NAEP scores in reading for 2011, while one point higher than in 2009, showed only 34 percent of eighth-grade students to be proficient or above (US Dept. of Education, NCES, 2011). Among students who took the ACT in preparation for applying to college, just over half, 51 percent, are able to meet the demands of college-level reading, based on ACT's national readiness indicator, and the percentage is substantially smaller for some groups, particularly male students;

African American, Hispanic, and Native American students; and students from families whose incomes are below $30,000 per year (ACT, 2006).

Perhaps more disturbing, despite the national focus on reading and literacy through the federal government initiatives No Child Left Behind and Race to the Top, we have indicators that rates of reading achievement have stagnated or fallen at the high school level in recent years. Program for International Student Assessment (PISA) scores in reading in the United States declined by four points between 2000 and 2010. ACT reading readiness measures in 2006 were at their lowest ebb in a decade. And tracking scores indicate that "more students are on track to being ready for college level reading in 8th and 10th grade than are actually ready by the time they reach 12th grade" (ACT, 2006, p. 1). This pattern of decline holds across both high and low achievers, with reports indicating that both dropouts and high school graduates are demonstrating significantly worse reading skills than in previous decades (USDOE, NCES, 2005).

The impact of these low reading achievement levels is felt on both individuals and the larger society. Every day, more than 3,000 students drop out of high school (Kamil, 2003); among the most commonly cited reasons for the dropout rate is that students don't have the reading skills to keep up with their coursework (Snow & Biancarosa, 2003). Eighty-two percent of prison inmates are high school dropouts, and more than one-third of juvenile offenders read below the fourth-grade level, an incarceration rate that drains an estimated $200 billion from the nation's economy in lost earnings and taxes (Coalition for Juvenile Justice, 2001). Of individuals who enter college, struggling readers are far less likely to complete a degree or certificate, with one study indicating a 70 percent dropout rate (Adelman, 2004). And employers consistently indicate a serious shortage of qualified employees, citing poor reading as a key reason (National Association of Manufacturers, Andersen, & the Center for Workforce Success, 2001). Even in the midst of the current economic downturn, half of companies surveyed describe finding qualified employees as a top business challenge (HireRight, 2011; Manpower Group, 2011).

Even for those of us who are fortunate to teach in classrooms or have children enrolled in schools where test scores are strong and graduation rates are high, it is hard to deny that academic reading achievement can be improved. As Margaret, a teacher at a high-achieving suburban high school commented, "I know my students are going to be okay in high school and probably even college; their parents will make sure of that. But will they have the skills to really achieve on their own in the long run? I don't know. They are sweet kids who have led pretty sheltered lives; I worry that they may not be fully prepared to compete in a world that is changing so quickly and that increasingly requires you to 'read the fine print.'"

"School" Reading

So why is there such a mismatch between reading demand and reading ability? Any parent who watches his or her middle or high school student lift a heavy backpack in the morning can tell you that the problem is not an absence of exposure to text; if anything, many students seem to be weighed down by the volume of their textbooks. A closer look, however, reveals that despite being surrounded by reading material, too few students are actually taught how to critically engage with complex texts in a manner that prepares them for the reading expectations of life after high school.

Research shows that to fully develop as competent and confident readers, secondary students need explicit instruction in reading well beyond the minimum level at which an individual is typically considered literate (Lyon, 2002; Moore, Bean, Birdyshaw, & Rycik, 1999). Indeed, the problem for struggling older readers is not illiteracy: the vast majority can decode and read at the word and sentence level, but they struggle to comprehend longer and more complex texts (Biancarosa & Snow, 2006). However, most schools do not explicitly teach reading beyond elementary or middle school.

Instead, instruction at the high school level is often focused more on content demands than on instruction in reading, a focus driven by both high-stakes testing and the traditional norms of teaching expectations, which assume that someone else "takes care of that"—a response that may sound familiar to you, and for good reason. According to one literacy expert, "Overwhelmed by higher content standards, many . . . high school teachers feel under pressure to 'cover' more content than ever before and resistant to 'adding' literacy responsibilities to their crowded course calendars. . . . Since literacy is not visible as a content area, it is not 'owned' by any department" (Meltzer, 2002, pp. 9–10). This lack of ownership extends across departments and often includes the one department that others assume is responsible, the English language arts department. As one educator notes, high school English teachers "are traditionally viewed—and view themselves—as outside the teaching of reading, because the assumption has been that students come to them knowing how to read," thereby allowing high school English classes to focus on literature rather than reading (Ericson, 2001, p. 1). As a high school history and later English teacher myself, I was certainly guilty of these beliefs. Early in my career, I assumed that my students should have been prepared with reading skills and strategies in middle school, and if they weren't, it was the middle school teachers' fault. I had a rude awakening when I took a job working in a middle school and realized that middle school teachers face the same pressures to cover content, and that while they often do work to teach reading skills, developing the necessary reading competencies requires more instruction than can be provided in elementary or middle school; it requires all of us working together across the grades, K–12.

Many of us also realize that the challenge of content instruction trumping reading opportunities is compounded by the reality that many students struggle to read complex discipline-based texts. Even textbooks, most of which are written at a middle school or upper-elementary reading level, prove too much for some students. This recognition leads many teachers to reduce or eliminate reading assignments altogether and instead present much of their material via PowerPoint or video, further diminishing opportunities for students to read and learn how to engage in meaningful interaction with texts while in high school (Rothman, 2012).

The focus on content learning is well intended; certainly we want students to graduate from high school with a well-developed understanding of core concepts from science, math, literature, history, and the arts. However, if we teach content knowledge without concurrently teaching students to read and critically respond to complex texts, we are limiting their potential for success in the workplace and in civic and community life and for ongoing disciplinary learning. To perform well in their jobs and be engaged citizens and community members, Hector, Lucy, Sara, and Craig need to have more than basic knowledge in their fields; they need to be able to access, interpret, analyze, evaluate, and apply new learning obtained through reading complex texts. Our schools must increasingly find ways to explicitly teach advanced reading skills, engage students with complex texts, and support disciplinary learning.

But how can teachers in various content areas accomplish this given all the pressures they face? In the pages that follow, read about how Kyra Lewis, a ninth-grade social studies teacher, has introduced a reading-for-learning model in her classroom.

Reading for Learning in the Middle and High School Classroom: An Example

With only a month of her semester-long geography course remaining, Kyra Lewis felt a mild panic begin to set in. Her ninth-grade students had explored much of the world and discussed geographic concepts such as location, place, and movement, but large chunks of knowledge were still missing. Kyra needed to ensure that students were exposed to concepts about political and economic geography, and they hadn't yet covered any material related to the largest and most populated continent, Asia. Despite all of this material to "get through," Kyra knew she didn't want to just lecture at her students. As a relatively new teacher, she had been surviving through energy, enthusiasm, and charisma, but Kyra could sense that her students were getting restless and she needed to find new ways to engage them in the material.

Dinner out with a college friend who had gone into the business world provided inspiration. As her friend described his work consulting for an international
client, Kyra's brain started popping with new possibilities for teaching and learning
in her classroom—and the "Where should we build a factory?" project was born.
After a busy weekend of researching and organizing, Kyra presented the project
to her students: Re-creating the kind of real-world reading and research that her
college friend did on a daily basis, she asked her students to take on the role of
consultants to a clothing manufacturer interested in locating a factory in one of
eight countries in Asia. To figure out which country would be the best fit for this
kind of company, her students, working in teams, researched information about the
infrastructure, political systems, political stability, manufacturing costs, workforce
readiness, economic policies, and human rights records of each country and then
make a recommendation to their client: Where should they locate their new factory and why? (See Figure 2.1.)

Allowing the project to drive the learning, Kyra encouraged students to begin
by brainstorming a list of questions that would help them with their task: Where

Figure 2.1. Kyra's introductory presentation slides for the Asia consulting project.

were these countries located? What is infrastructure and why is it important? How do you determine political stability? What are the different political systems and why do they matter to a factory? What kinds of things should be counted toward manufacturing costs? As students brainstormed the list, Kyra held her tongue, resisting the urge to provide answers and instead encouraging the students to think next about where they might find information that could help them to develop their own solutions. She then pointed them toward classroom materials and online resources and challenged them to read, research, and continue asking questions.

Over the following weeks, both the students and their teacher read and learned a lot. The students found out about railroads in India, compared the GDP and GNP of Thailand, considered education levels versus labor costs in Japan, and reviewed competing perspectives on the human rights record of China. They learned to navigate between different sources of information, discovered the possibilities and limitations of Wikipedia, developed strategies for uncovering author and publisher biases, strengthened their ability to annotate and take notes efficiently, and figured out how to approach and make meaning from complex and challenging texts.

Kyra, meanwhile, learned when to step in to provide information and when to allow students to experience the discomfort of ambiguity and the reward of finding answers on their own. She became a master of the ten-minute mini-lesson, providing targeted demonstrations and pared-down lectures on topics that emerged from regular check-ins she held with each student group, lessons that ranged from the difference between communism and capitalism to honing the key words for an Internet search. And she learned to listen. "I thought I knew my students before," Kyra commented,

> but as we worked through this unit, I realized how much I didn't know. They are really smart and capable of much more than I had given them credit for. At the same time, they have some significant gaps in their skill sets, particularly around reading and research. The regular check-ins that I held with each consulting group helped me to understand how to target my teaching to ensure that they developed the skills they needed for success.

At the end of the semester, teams of student consultants, dressed in their finest "business" attire, presented their recommendations to panels of teachers, administrators, and business professionals from the local community. Their answers to the question of where to locate the factory varied; several teams recommended India, citing a relatively low cost of labor, increasingly educated populace, and democratically elected government that was an ally of the United States. Others argued that China presented a similarly educated populace with a more stable political system that, although communist, had proved friendly to international manufacturing. Still others argued in favor of the Philippines, Vietnam, or Thailand, citing justifications that demonstrated a range of knowledge of current events, government structures, economic policies, natural resources, and international trade. There was no one right answer; the possibilities were many, and students' success was measured by the thoroughness of their research and the thoughtfulness of their analysis (see Figure 2.2).

Many of the presentations were halting at first, but as students realized just how much they knew, their recommendations and explanations became increasingly confident. During the Q&A portion of the presentations, students fielded questions that further demonstrated the depth of their knowledge and their awareness of their learning. "I didn't even know where these countries were when Ms. Lewis first told us about the project," one student admitted, "but now I feel like I

Figure 2.2. Students' "Where in Asia should we build a factory?" presentation posters.

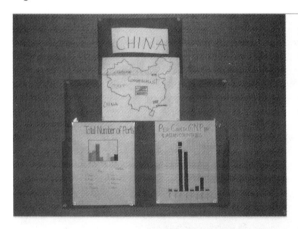
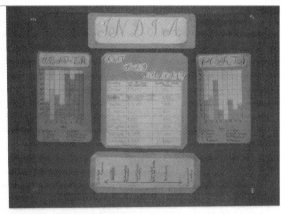
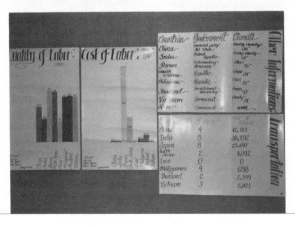

know more about them than most adults. They were discussing Laos on the news the other day and I was able to tell my parents about what was happening and why it was important." Another student reflected that she had never voluntarily read so much before. "I usually just skim over the assignment," she acknowledged, "but on this project we kept coming up with more questions and having to look for more information. It was definitely hard, but now I feel like I am better prepared for college and have skills I can actually use in the real world."

Unpacking the Consulting Project: Characteristics of Reading for Learning

Throughout the consulting project, students in Kyra's class were involved in purposeful and meaningful reading. They read a wide diversity of materials, ranging from their textbook to online reference materials to news articles found on Twitter feeds to high-level analyses of human rights abuses and economic policies. If Kyra had set these materials in front of students and simply told them to read, many, if not all, of her students would likely have resisted. In this project, however, the students surprised both their teacher and themselves with the breadth and the depth of their reading accomplishments. What was different this time? A close analysis of the design and structure of teaching and learning during the consulting project reveals the characteristics of real-world reading in the high school classroom listed in Figure 2.3.

Discipline-Driven Reading

The reading that students do in school needs to reflect the kinds of reading that people do in the world outside of school. In the world beyond high school, people read when they need to answer real questions in response to real problems. They approach texts in different ways, depending on their discipline and their purpose. They might read bits of multiple texts that respond to a specific concern or spend time examining a single article in depth, seeking to understand its details, biases, and implications. They will skim some texts quickly but read other texts multiple times as they develop new questions, delve more deeply into problems, and recognize the need to gather more information or consider alternative perspectives.

In school, however, we often expect students to approach texts in a nearly uniform manner across all of their courses. They read from a single source, the textbook, and the purpose is nearly always about acquiring information. The assignment often requires that students read linearly, from the beginning to the end—though in truth, many students skim and scan to answer the questions required of them in as short a time (and with as little intellectual engagement) as

---

Figure 2.3. Instructional strategies that support reading for learning in the disciplines.

- **Discipline-Driven Reading**

  ○ Ask real questions. Assign readings that help students respond to those questions.

  ○ Teach students to read purposefully and to differentiate their approach to respond to their purpose and the demands of the text.

  ○ Teach students to read critically and to approach texts in a manner that reflects the demands of the discipline.

- **Complex Texts**

  ○ Move beyond the textbook to expose students to reading multiple types of print and electronic texts.

  ○ Challenge students to read more complex texts that are authentic to the discipline.

  ○ Use scaffolding and collaboration to support students in reading more complex texts.

- **Embedded and Responsive Strategy Instruction**

  ○ Provide "just-in-time" instruction in research and reading strategies to support students in accessing, comprehending, and analyzing texts.

  ○ Use short mini-lessons to build background knowledge or model reading practices appropriate to the discipline.

  ○ Monitor student progress through conferences, observations, and informal assessments to better understand strengths and needs.

- **Practice, Practice, Practice**

  ○ Provide multiple opportunities and structures for students to read a wide variety of texts.

  ○ Dedicate time in class for students to read and respond to texts appropriate to the topic and discipline.

---

possible. This approach limits students' preparation for the real-world reading demands of work and civic life, and it also limits their understanding of the disciplines.

Every subject that we teach in school, from history to science, math to literature, is more than a collection of facts and skills; our disciplines represent distinctive ways of knowing and thinking. Sam Wineburg (2001), a scholar in history education, devoted his dissertation research to investigating the ways in which historians and laypeople approach primary source documents in history. In presenting his findings, he compares the approaches to those of a prosecuting attorney versus a jury. The historian "interrogates" the documents, actively analyzing and questioning the texts and their authors to seek to understand motivations, biases, and context for the materials. The layperson, on the other hand, treats the materials as a more passive jury might in approaching a witness in a courtroom: listening carefully, taking notes, but unable to directly engage with the material. If we want our students to truly understand the discipline of history, it is not enough to teach them the "facts" about the past, particularly since the facts are so often under dispute. We must teach them to become active interrogators in their readings and interactions with texts. Wineburg and his colleagues at the Stanford History Education Group (http://sheg.stanford.edu) encourage teaching students to engage with historical documents using sourcing, contextualizing, corroborating, and close reading strategies—all strategies designed to help young readers develop the dispositions and understandings that are responsive to the disciplinary fields of history and the social sciences and that are also necessary to be effective participants in many professional and civic roles. If we want students to understand the disciplines of science, mathematics, literature, language, engineering, and the arts, we must similarly uncover the discipline-specific approaches to reading that are inherent in these content areas and provide students with opportunities to approximate them in our classrooms.

In this unit, Kyra provided her ninth-grade geography students with opportunities to read like social scientists, economists, and business professionals. Rather than telling them what to read, she provided them with an authentic, open-ended problem and, with guidance and support, encouraged them to locate and engage with texts that allowed them to explore potential answers. Students were expected to ask questions that gave purpose to their reading, to consider the sources and biases of each text, to compare information from multiple sources, and to apply their learning back to the analysis of the original problem. At the same time, they were also allowed to skip around in their readings, to locate the most relevant materials, and to discard a text if it wasn't helpful. In short, their reading process required them to be active thinkers and to take responsibility for their own learning.

At first, students were somewhat intimidated by the open-ended nature of the project. Many, accustomed to much more teacher-directed work, felt unsure about how to respond. Kyra responded to students' anxiety with patience, lots of modeling, and plenty of individual and small-group support. "We spent a lot of time working together to brainstorm the kinds of questions they should be researching, discuss strategies for reading the texts, and identify the 'red flags' they should look for when analyzing texts." Kyra taught skill-focused mini-lessons at the beginning of most class periods and brought students back together at the end of the period

Teaching Tip

If you are asking students to read and research on their own, it can be helpful to create a set of prese-lected discipline- and topic-appropriate materials to help them get started. If your students are online, use digital curation sites like Diigo and Scoop.it to organize resources. If you don't yet have access to computers or mobile devices, then binders, folders, and milk crates are low-tech resources that can be used for similar purposes. In the spirit of creating a collaborative learning community, encourage students to contribute to the collection as they find resources.

to debrief and problem-solve. She also invited professional consultants and business analysts who do similar work into the classroom to share their experiences. "The guest speakers made a big difference for the students. They provided some great context and helped make the project real for the kids. Plus, the students knew that these same speakers were coming back to hear their presentations. It was a big incentive to keep working and persevere, even when the reading and research was hard."

With guidance and support, students grew in confidence and were soon ready to take ownership of their reading choices. "It felt strange in the beginning because it was like 'hey, you are the teacher, shouldn't you be telling us what to read?'" one student commented. "But Ms. Lewis told us that since we were the consultants, we had to figure out what information we needed and what we should read to find that information out. That made it a lot more difficult in some ways. I had to work a lot harder on this project than I usually do. With everything we read, we had to think about, was it relevant? Did it contain helpful information? Who wrote it? What were the biases? How did it connect with other information? How can I use the information? Some days I felt like it made my brain hurt. But I feel like I learned a lot more and I have a lot more confidence that I could do something like this in the future."

Complex Texts

"One of my biggest concerns going into this project," Kyra admits, "is that the students weren't going to be able to read the materials." According to their previous standardized test scores, the majority of Kyra's students read below or significantly below grade level. Many of the materials that students would need to access and interpret in order to respond to the problem were at or above grade level. Although the textbook was one available resource, most texts that students would access were written for out-of-school audiences and did not consistently contain headings, predictable structures, jargon-free language, or other comprehension elements typical of considerate texts (Armbruster & Anderson, 1981). Looking around the classroom on a typical day during this unit, you could see some students online reading country reports created by the US State Department; others sat together perusing business journals and trade magazine articles about economic trends in Asia; still others compared year-over-year charts of market trends that one of the guest speakers had provided to the class. Some of these texts were preselected by Kyra and available to students through the class website, others were independently identified by students through online searches and database investigations, while others were specific recommendations from Kyra to individual students or student teams based on their interests and reading abilities.

Many of these texts were messy and complex. They contained complicated ideas. Some were written in a style that was more technical or academic than these ninth graders were used to. The texts often assumed significant prior knowledge about a topic. And some were unreliable. But they also represented the kind of reading that is expected outside of school, where a teacher isn't usually available to act as an intermediary between the text and the student and the reader must determine how to navigate the material for him- or herself. And, as research tells us, performance with complex texts has been shown to be the clearest differentiator between students who meet college readiness benchmarks and those who do not (ACT, 2006). Students who could read and understand complex texts consistently performed higher than their peers regardless of race, ethnicity, gender, or family income level (see Figure 2.4).

Research has also indicated that exposure to multiple texts that are authentic to a discipline is critical for building content understanding (Brozo & Hargis, 2003). This holds at all levels from kindergarten through college. Nichols (2009) found that even elementary school children significantly benefited from "layering" texts; engaging students in multiple readings on the same topic enabled students to build deep conceptual understanding.

In Kyra's classroom, students rose to the occasion. Despite the challenges inherent in the texts, for the most part they were able to navigate the complex materials. Several factors contributed to their success. First, students were motivated to read the material because they were interested in the real-world nature of the project. Intrinsic motivation contributes significantly to students' ability to successfully navigate challenges (Deci, 1996). Having a project that demanded they answer a real question for a real audience inspired even some of the most reluctant students to step up and engage with the texts. Second, students had a clear purpose for reading each text. Knowing what they wanted to get out of a specific text and being able to select specific portions of the text to read more closely supported their comprehension (Bransford, Brown, & Cocking, 2000). Kyra worked with students through whole-group mini-lessons as well as individual and small-group conferences to teach them how to set a purpose for reading the text. For many this was a new skill. They were accustomed to having the teacher tell them what to read and why. Adapting to taking ownership of their reading selections and purpose for reading was challenging. To help the process along, Kyra posted a series of guiding

Figure 2.4. Recognizing complex texts.

There are many definitions of *complex texts*. The Common Core State Standards define *text complexity* through three dimensions:

- Quantitative: This includes variables such as word length or frequency, sentence length, and cohesion.
- Qualitative: This concerns levels of meaning in the text, clarity of language, and prior knowledge demands.
- Reader–Text Interaction: This dimension concerns reader motivation, knowledge, and experience. (CCSS, 2012, Appendix A)

In its policy research brief *Reading Instruction for All Students,* NCTE notes that both the qualitative and especially the reader–text dimensions of the CCSS definition are highly dependent on the professional judgment of teachers because "only teachers know students well enough to help them find the best text for the purpose at hand, something 'leveling' systems cannot do" (NCTE, 2012, p. 1).

Another widely used description of complex texts comes from ACT, which defines more complex texts as having the following "RSVP" characteristics:

- Relationships—Interactions among ideas or characters in the texts are subtle, involved, or deeply embedded.
- Richness—The text possesses a sizeable amount of highly sophisticated information conveyed through data or literary devices.
- Structure—The text is organized in ways that are elaborate and sometimes unconventional.
- Style—The author's tone and use of language are often intricate.
- Vocabulary—The author's choice of words is demanding and highly context dependent.
- Purpose—The author's intent in writing the text is implicit and sometimes ambiguous. (ACT, 2006, p. 17).

questions at the front of the room: "What are you reading? (Title, author, source) What do you expect to learn from it? (Information, ideas, perspectives) How will it help you answer your research question?" (see Figure 2.5). Finally, students were supported throughout the process by the opportunity to collaborate and check for understanding among their peers. Because they were working in teams, students were able to talk with their classmates, sharing information, seeking agreement, and working together to make sense of seemingly contradictory findings. When students can talk about their reading, comprehension increases and retention of information is strengthened (Cawelti, 2004; Marzano, Pickering, & Pollock, 2001).

The complex texts students read during this project were not easy. Students sometimes found themselves rereading materials multiple times. They made good use of Dictionary.com and similar apps on their smartphones and the classroom computers. Occasionally, students needed to be reminded that it was okay to supplement or replace a text if it was just too difficult. However, all of these

---

Figure 2.5. Setting a purpose for reading.

SETTING A PURPOSE FOR READING:

① What are you reading?
  (Title, author, source)

② What do you expect to learn from it?
  (information, ideas, perspectives)

③ How will it help you answer your research question?

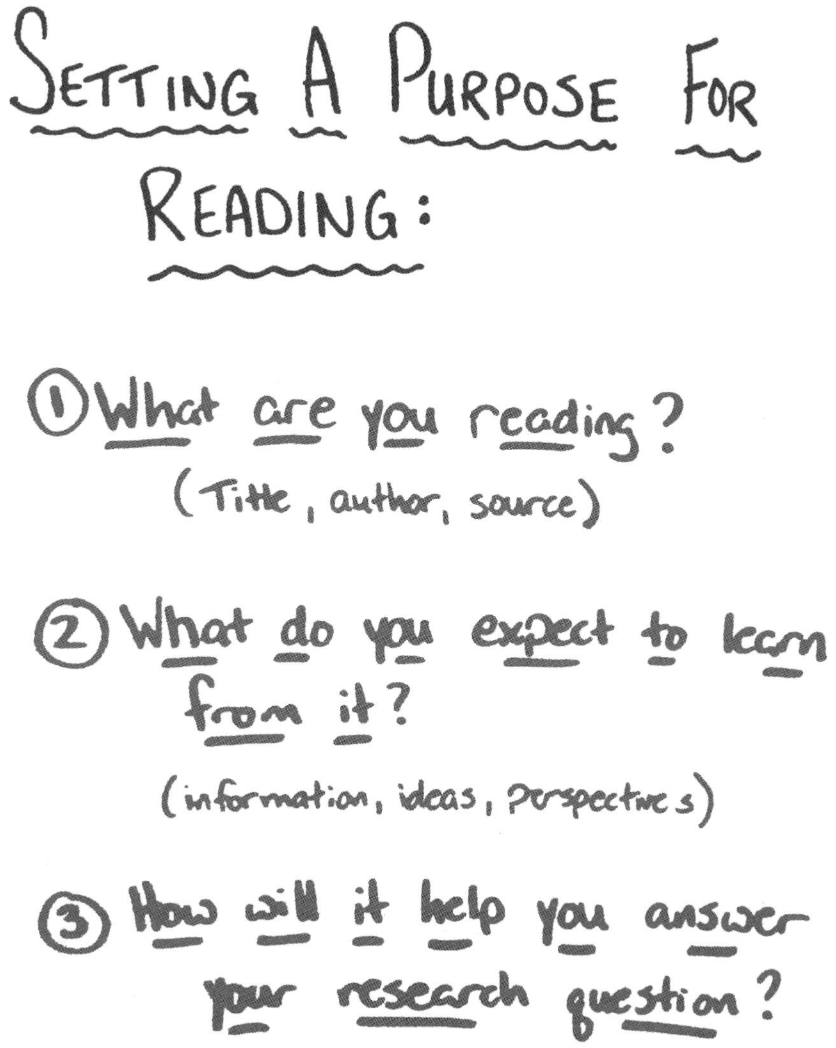

experiences provided students with a more nuanced understanding of the content of, as well as practice with, the skills and strategies they would need to navigate complex texts beyond the high school classroom. Literacy expert Sheridan Blau (2003) has stated that if students aren't confronted with challenging new information, ideas, and ways of thinking, then the material they are reading isn't difficult enough. Having guided her students through the consulting project, Kyra firmly agrees: "I was amazed by what the students were able to read in this unit. Before, I thought I was helping them by sheltering them from more challenging texts, but now I realize that I wasn't doing them any favors. In the right circumstances, they can handle more complex readings, and they need to be pushed."

Embedded and Responsive Strategy Instruction

Another factor critical to the success of the "Where should we build a factory?" project was Kyra's use of targeted instruction in discipline-based reading and research strategies. By carefully monitoring students' progress, Kyra was able to anticipate some challenges and immediately recognize areas where students were struggling. She supported students' learning by regularly teaching short mini-lessons that responded to areas where students needed support. These lessons ranged from modeling strategies for skimming and scanning through the text, to identifying relevant information, to enumerating key items to look for when evaluating bias in online resources. Some lessons provided background information on topics such as political and economic terminology to help build a conceptual framework, or schema, that would support comprehension as students encountered new information about country-specific political structures and economic policies in their readings (Jensen, 2005; Sousa, 2001). Other lessons consisted of a facilitated brainstorming session in which students could share their challenges and successes and problem-solve together.

Building on the mini-lesson model advocated by Atwell (1998) and Calkins (2001), Kyra kept her instruction short and focused. "Most of the lessons lasted only ten to fifteen minutes and addressed only one specific strategy," she explained.

> If they went much longer, students tended to lose focus. I found that for mini-lessons to be successful they needed to follow the "just-in-time" approach—responding to what students needed at that stage of their research. And then I needed to get out

of the way to let [students] apply the learning to what they were doing. Of course, I didn't go too far, since some students would inevitably need more support or further explanation, but that was more effective done individually or in small groups while others got on with their work.

On the best days, these mini-lesson sessions felt like the morning meeting of a consulting group, with team members coming together to check in with the project manager, get advice on new approaches, share ideas, and prepare for the work ahead.

A wealth of research and resources describe reading strategies that students can use to strengthen comprehension and content understanding (see, for example, Allington, 2005; Keene & Zimmerman, 2007; Harvey & Goudvis, 2007). Suggested strategies include monitoring com-

> ## Teaching Tip
>
> Doing the reading and research alongside your students can help you anticipate some of the challenges and opportunities they might encounter. These challenges and opportunities can then become the focus of mini-lessons, limiting frustration for both students and teacher.

prehension, using text features, asking questions, and making connections. These strategies are often used unconsciously by strong readers, and research has found that explicit instruction in the strategies can help struggling readers to succeed (Allington, 2005). Programs such as Reading Recovery and Striving Readers embrace these strategies as a core organizing principle. However, strategy instruction need not be limited to intervention programs. Indeed, it is often much more powerful when embedded within a larger project, where it can be immediately applied to meaningful reading tasks that have relevance beyond simply strengthening comprehension skills. Further, since the strategies that are necessary to read a primary source history document are distinct from the strategies that are necessary to read a more procedurally focused science text, for example, targeted instruction is required for students across the reading spectrum. By embedding instruction where it could respond to "just-in-time" needs, Kyra taught her students critical reading and research skills while also demonstrating the need and relevance for applying and mastering those skills.

Practice, Practice, Practice

The best way to strengthen students' ability to read is to give them plenty of opportunities to read. Time spent reading, both in and out of school, is consistently linked to stronger reading scores, greater reading confidence, and greater interest in and enthusiasm for reading, which, in turn, leads to more reading. In this consulting unit, students had multiple opportunities to read. They read online as well as hard copies of text. They read on their own and they read collaboratively.

Teaching Tip

If you are struggling to find the time in class to read, it can be helpful to broaden the definition of *text*. Photos, infographics, diagrams, videos, and even lectures can be all be considered texts. Build disciplinary thinking skills by teaching students to approach these materials with the same critical reading lens they apply to more traditional printed materials.

They read some texts from start to finish but read others in chunks. They read materials they had self-selected and they read materials that were suggested by the teacher. They read their textbook and Wikipedia for background information, and they read more academically rigorous texts to flesh out their understanding and respond to more specific questions. In short, they read—a lot. In her end-of-project self-evaluation, one student reflected, "I read more for this project than I did for the rest of the semester in all my other classes. Combined!!!!!"

Critically, a significant portion of the reading for this project was done in class. One of the advantages of crafting instruction into short mini-lessons is that it allows time during the rest of the period for students to engage in reading, research, and collaboration. This workshop structure not only provides students with opportunities to apply their learning with teacher support, but it also demonstrates the importance of the reading and research process. When we relegate reading and research to homework, we implicitly communicate the message that these literacy activities are not as important as the lectures, worksheets, or tests carried out in class. However, we know that the act of reading, especially when structured in response to an open-ended question such as provided in the consulting project, is a cognitive task that demands thinking and promotes disciplinary learning. If we are to demonstrate the primacy of reading, we need to dedicate time during class for students to read.

Kyra readily acknowledges that when she first started using time in class for students to read and research, she worried that students, parents, colleagues, and her principal would think she was shirking her duties. "The image of the teacher is that she is the one at the front of the room lecturing, especially in a history class. As a fairly new teacher, I worried that there would be repercussions if I didn't live up to that ideal." At first she kept her door closed, but later, as the students started to take off with the project, they needed more space to work and so moved into the corridor outside the classroom, to the library, and even to the outdoor patio to work. At that point, Kyra couldn't keep her approach a secret any longer. "Fortunately, no one yelled at me," she laughs. "Instead I had colleagues coming up and asking what I was doing with the students that kept them so engaged." Of course, district benchmarks and state standardized tests were an ever-present concern as well, but in the end, Kyra needn't have worried. Her students scored higher on the test than their peers at many of the other schools in the district and did particularly well on the test questions relevant to the material addressed by the consulting project. By beginning the unit design with a focus and question that derived from core areas in her discipline, Kyra was able to carve out the time needed to truly engage her students in disciplinary learning in the classroom, emphasizing authentic reading and research opportunities while also teaching the core content.

Classroom Portraits of Reading for Learning

After the last student group had presented the results of its consulting project and the guest panelists had gone home, Kyra breathed a sigh of relief. The project, she admitted, had been exhausting, and she was glad for the long weekend ahead to recover. Would she do it again? "Absolutely!" she immediately replied. "It was so worth it to see the growth in the students. They did things that none of us imagined they could do. I watched students who struggle with English locate, read, and analyze articles from *The Economist*. I heard some of my toughest kids debating human rights and the ethical responsibilities of corporations." She laughed. "Now I just need to figure out how to create similar learning experiences for the other topics I teach."

The following sections describe examples that demonstrate how other teachers have created similar opportunities to engage students in meaningful, discipline-based reading across a range of content areas and grade levels. The teaching and learning varies with the discipline, the students' needs, and the teacher's style. However, all strive to approximate the experience and demands of reading and learning beyond high school—in college, career, and community and civic life. As you read, consider how each of the characteristics described in Figure 2.3 and for Kyra's consulting project applies to the example profiled. And then consider how you might apply the questions in the following list to reading opportunities in your own classroom.

- **Discipline-Driven Reading.** Are students asked to use readings to respond to an open-ended, real-world problem? Do the readings promote discipline-specific ways of thinking?

- **Complex Texts.** Are students engaged with varied and complex texts? Are the texts authentic to the discipline?

- **Embedded and Responsive Strategy Instruction.** How can targeted instruction support students by providing immediate access to text as well as helping them to develop long-term reading and research skills and strategies? How can assessment be used to ensure that strategy instruction is responsive to students' strengths and needs?

- **Practice, Practice, Practice.** Do students have multiple opportunities to engage with a wide range of texts? Are students given time to read during the school day?

The Organ Donor Project

Each spring students in Wendy Li's biology class partner with a local hospital to create a multimedia campaign for organ donor awareness month in April. The project begins with a presentation by doctors and organ donation advocates, who explain that thousands of people are waiting for organ transplants that will significantly improve, extend, or save their lives. They describe the difficulty in recruiting organ donors and the urgent need for more education and awareness. The students are then put into teams, each of which is responsible for creating a multimedia campaign focused on a specific type of organ donation, including kidney, bone marrow, eye, heart, lungs, and skin. Teams are tasked with researching information on the harvesting and transplant process and then presenting their findings in a way that is engaging, informative, and compelling. The best campaigns are featured on the hospital's website, and in recent years some have even been broadcast on local radio and television.

As you might imagine, reading is a huge focus of this project. Although the class explores general information on human physiology before beginning the project, the specifics of how different organs interact within their body system, concerns around immune response and rejection, possibilities for transplanting organs from living donors, demands for harvesting organs from deceased donors, and technical details about how organs can be surgically transplanted vary significantly among organ types. Each team spends a lot of time reading and researching to find out the specifics for their organ. The fact that students are working with a hospital adds to the sense of urgency. As one student commented, "The doctors are going to be looking at our work. We can't fake facts that we don't know."

The need for accurate and detailed information means that students often plunge into medical reference texts. Wendy, once a pre-med student herself before finding her calling as a teacher, brings into class her college biology and physiology texts, and the hospital loans the class materials from its reference library, including the classic volume for all first-year medical students, *Gray's Anatomy* (which many students are surprised to learn existed long before the television series came into being).

These texts are difficult and require significant support for student success. Wendy scaffolds students' reading by providing general background information on topics such as body systems and immune response and general tips on how to use the various text supports (such as headings and indexes to find relevant information). She also shares tips that she found helpful when reading similarly detailed reference texts as a pre-med student.

I teach the students to start with the diagrams. In medical books, they are often really detailed and really helpful. If you can wrap your mind around the diagrams first, then it is often much easier to make meaning from the text itself. I also teach them not to be afraid of looking up words. There is so much jargon in medical texts. I keep a sticky note in the glossary so that I can get there easily and a notepad next to the book so that I can create my own list of definitions for the part of the text that I'm reading.

Students' research is also supported by face-to-face and email check-ins with doctors from the sponsoring hospital. The medical professionals answer questions, clear up confusion, and provide examples from their experience to supplement students' research. Additionally, they provide encouragement and reassurance about the challenge of this work, telling students, "Medicine is like learning a whole new language." During the final presentations, students often surprise themselves as they demonstrate the depth of their learning and their proficiency in this "new language." Terms that just a few weeks earlier were hard to pronounce roll off their tongues as they share their multimedia campaigns with their audience. Wendy always feels tremendous pride watching students present, but her favorite images of students engaged in the organ donor project come earlier in the investigation. "I love it when the students are working in their groups with three or four different medical reference texts open around them and they are sitting there taking notes and discussing the details with each other. When I see that, I flash forward a few years and imagine these awkward adolescents as medical students or doctors someday. I just hope that the skills they are learning today will position them well if they choose to go down that path."

Author Podcast Project

Independent reading is a huge push in Jennifer Cramer's eleventh-grade American literature class. Most of her students arrive reading below grade level, and Jennifer is well aware that her class may be one of the last opportunities to shore up reading skills and hook these students into reading for pleasure. Recognizing that reading literature is a true lifelong learning opportunity—a way to escape pressing realities, imagine new worlds, build empathy for others, and strengthen language use—Jennifer chooses to dedicate a portion of her class time every week to independent reading. She maintains a huge classroom library full of popular young adult books, subscribes to listservs that provide ideas for the next big thing in YA lit, scrounges sales and coupon deals for more books, gives weekly author talks designed to "sell" new authors and book titles, and is continually reading to update her own familiarity with the field. Her efforts yield results: her students report being more interested in reading and doing more reading outside of class; test scores reveal an increase in reading skills; and over the course of the year, most students significantly broaden and deepen the range of genres, authors, and subjects they choose to read independently.

Of course, this being a course in American literature, Jennifer's students are also reading the expected canon of Hemingway, Steinbeck, Fitzgerald, and Miller. They read, analyze, discuss, and then write the district benchmark essay. Jennifer employs multiple strategies to make the required reading engaging, but she often feels that there is a disconnect between the kind of reading experience her students encounter in independent reading versus the experience they have wading through *The Crucible* or *The Great Gatsby*. "I try to help them see the connections between the analysis we do with the classics and what they can apply to their independent reading, but most just don't see the relevance of analyzing the author's intent or looking for evidence of foreshadowing. The kids are great and they want to be supportive, but sometimes they get frustrated and ask, 'When am I ever going to use this?'"

A few years ago, Jennifer stumbled on a solution to help build a bridge between the seemingly disparate reading experiences students encountered in her classroom. She was preparing to go on maternity leave the following fall and was concerned that during her time away, her incoming students would need support to get hooked into independent reading. Not sure that she could rely on a substitute to have the background in YA lit needed to provide book recommendations and author talks to her new students, she asked her current students to help create a series of podcasts that featured their favorite authors. Together they brainstormed the elements that should go into a successful author talk. They decided that the talk needed to provide information on the full scope of the author's work while also featuring a few favorite texts with details that could grab prospective readers' attention; should include a discussion of the author's style, perspective, common themes, and target audience; and needed to be fun, engaging, and personable while also providing text-specific evidence that would allow prospective readers to make good decisions about whether a book was a good fit for them.

Jennifer then tasked students with the challenge of revisiting some of their favorite independent reading texts with a more critical lens. Rather than simply reading for pleasure, they were now reading as reviewers—considering why the book had affected them and how it might be received by others. They read additional works by the same author and began noting similarities in the author's style and tone, common themes that emerged across texts, and subtle differences in character and plot that allowed each text to stand on its own. They carefully chose specific text evidence that they felt would best represent the author's approach in their podcasts and then practiced reading aloud to ensure fluency and determine the best use of tone and inflection.

Watching them at work, Jennifer realized that the students were, on their own, applying all of the skills they had been working on throughout the year with the required literature.

> It was fantastic to see them digging more deeply into the texts, to recognize the complexity that the reading had to offer, and to apply the analytical skills that we'd been working on since September but that I don't think they'd really realized they had developed. I had to smile when I'd hear students use terms like *author's craft, story arc,* or *stylistic devices* in their podcasts. They had so often groaned when I used the terms with *Gatsby* or *Scarlet Letter,* but now they were using them on their own.

Initially, Jennifer wondered if the students worked so hard on their podcasts out of loyalty to her and support for her new baby. But when she came back from maternity leave the following November, she realized that their efforts hadn't really been about her at all. When her former students, now seniors, came to visit, their first questions were often not about the baby but instead about the podcasts: "Did your new students listen to my podcast? Did they like it? What books are they reading? Are they reading my author?" Creating podcasts for an authentic audience of readers who were just like them, only a little younger, provided Jennifer's students with a genuine reason to read, analyze, and interpret literature. This work wasn't just another boring district benchmark; this was something that would be listened to by people they knew and whose respect they cared about. Students wanted their work to be good and to have an impact, and it was this desire that propelled them to engage in the type of analytical reading of literature that is authentic to the discipline.

Today, author podcasts are a key component of the literature-rich environment in Jennifer's classroom. Students engage with the podcasts as both creators and audience members. Although she continues to give author talks to provide models and expand students' repertoire, Jennifer has found there is real strength in allowing the students to recommend books to one another through the podcasts.

> It engages them on so many levels. When searching for new books, they are sometimes more willing to take recommendations from their peers than they are from me. When creating a podcast, they dig deeper into the books and think more critically as readers and writers. The fact that we've been doing this for three years now means that we have quite a collection, so some of the kids are more willing to challenge themselves to find new authors to review, or sometimes they'll engage in a virtual conversation with another reviewer by doing a follow-up podcast that offers an alternative perspective. As a teacher, I love that there are now so many more voices in the conversation. It is no longer just me reviewing books and giving recommendations. We've now become a true community of readers.

Hairspray Theater Production

Sam Jacobsen's advanced theater students were thrilled when it was announced that they would be performing *Hairspray* for the winter musical. Most had seen the movie or heard the music, but as they began preparations it became very clear that many were completely unfamiliar with the context of 1960s Baltimore. At first Sam attempted to answer students' questions, but as they moved from read-through into auditions and production, it was evident that students needed more information than he was able to provide. This was a student-led production class in which students were expected to take on set design, costumes, and choreography as well as all of the stage roles. Since a major goal of the class was to provide students with an authentic theater experience, Sam decided they should research the production in the same way that professionals are expected to do. Students would become responsible for learning the history and context of the play in order to create a production that was responsive to the place and time in which *Hairspray* is set.

The class began the research process by drawing up a list of questions: How segregated was Baltimore in the 1960s? What were the laws around segregation in Maryland? How long had TV been around? What did TV dance shows look like? What was the first TV dance show to integrate? What was happening with integration in other forms of media and sports? Were schools segregated as well? What was popular opinion about race and segregation at the time? What about the roles of women? What did women wear in the 1960s and how did that reflect gender expectations? How did issues around race, class, and gender in Baltimore compare to the rest of the country?

Sam invited a history teacher colleague to visit the class to act as an "expert consultant" to the stage production team. The teacher-consultant provided a general background on the time period, offered initial answers to questions, and gave suggestions about where students might go to find more information. The interaction also gave students a glimpse into the individual woman who was a history teacher for many of these students in another period of their school day. In that role, she was "just a teacher," but as a consultant for this project, she "knew so much!"

The students divided into collaborative research teams reflecting both their research interests and their roles in the production. The lead costume design team, for example, researched clothing styles and gender roles in the 1960s, while the choreography team researched popular dance styles and restrictions on social interactions between African American and white teens. Students initially looked for information in reference texts and historical materials, but then a librarian suggested they expand their search to include popular magazines from the sixties. The visual imagery, language style, intended audience, and diverse collection of articles and advertisements in these materials proved an incredible resource for helping students understand the feel of the time and provided them with great references to use in designing their own production. Unfortunately, the school library had access to few of these primary sources, but the downtown public library and the local university library had great collections, and weekends found many of these students immersed in old issues of *Life* and *Ebony* magazines.

While the students researched, plans for production began, with students beginning to run lines, block out the staging, and design scenery and costumes. Time was valuable, as it always is when a production deadline is looming, but Sam decided to dedicate the first ten to fifteen minutes of most class meetings to having students share the findings from their research. Student research teams were assigned specific days to present what they had learned and to discuss its relevance to the class production. These presentations often led to thoughtful discussions, with "aha" moments as the actors came to better understand the motivations and context behind their character's lines. "I never really understood why my character was so worried that her son was dating a white girl until I heard one of the other groups present about some of the hate crimes from that time. I thought of Baltimore as more of a northern city. I didn't realize that the Klan had tentacles everywhere." The feedback sessions also gave Sam a chance to listen in on his students' thinking, correct any misconceptions that were developing through their research process, ask a few probing questions to push their thinking, and ensure that they were applying their new learning to the stage production.

"Are we going to have to write a research paper on this?" This question, voiced by one of Sam's students, had been hovering in the back of many of their minds. After all, their previous research experiences had taught them that an academic paper was the inevitable outcome of any investigation. But a theater production team doesn't often write research papers. Instead, they apply their learning to the production by designing props, costumes, and scenery and making acting choices about tone, action, and character interaction that respond to the time and location of the play. As the production came together, Sam could see the depth of students' knowledge in the musical's details. From the women's hairstyles to the intonations in the actors' voices, it was clear that students had developed a nuanced understanding of 1960s Baltimore.

To ensure that the audience appreciated these details as well, Sam decided to hold an Actors Studio–style Q&A after the production on opening night, inviting the audience to stay after the curtain fell so that the students could share their experiences and answer any questions the production raised. Both students and teacher were nervous, knowing that several local theater directors as well as teachers and parents would be in attendance. But the students did a fantastic job, earning high praise from the audience and gaining confidence in their own voices. "People were really interested," one student commented later. "I've done lots of productions, and its always great getting the applause and knowing you've done a good job in your role, so I wasn't sure about going out after as myself to share research. But answering questions and sharing our story made me feel like I have something to say. It made me realize how much I learned."

Connection to the Common Core State Standards

The instructional principles described in this chapter respond directly to the reading expectations set forth in the Common Core State Standards (CCSS). Like the CCSS, the teaching approaches described here are born out of a concern that students be prepared for the world of work, higher education, and civic and community life when they complete twelfth grade. In particular, note in the following standards the inclusion of the demands that students integrate and evaluate content from diverse formats and media, evaluate argument and claims, and read and understand complex texts. Designing instruction that engages students in reading to promote disciplinary thinking, utilizes varied and complex texts, provides embedded and responsive strategy instruction, and allows regular opportunities to read across grade level and content area supports the development of these skills and understandings as required by the CCSS.

College and Career Readiness Anchor Standards for Reading, Grades 6–12

Key Ideas and Details

1. Read closely to determine what the text says explicitly and to make logical inferences from it; cite specific textual evidence when writing or speaking to support conclusions drawn from text.
2. Determine central ideas or themes of a text and analyze their development; summarize the key supporting details and ideas.
3. Analyze how and why individuals, events, and ideas develop and interact over the course of a text.

Craft and Structure

4. Interpret words and phrases as they are used in a text, including determining technical, connotative, and figurative meanings, and analyze how specific word choices shape meaning or tone.
5. Analyze the structure of texts, including how specific sentences, paragraphs, and larger portions of the text (e.g., a section, chapter, scene, or stanza) relate to each other and the whole.
6. Assess how point of view or purpose shapes the content and style of a text.

Integration of Knowledge and Ideas

7. Integrate and evaluate content presented in diverse formats and media, including visually and quantitatively, as well as in words.
8. Delineate and evaluate the argument and specific claims in a text, including the validity of the reasoning as well as the relevance and sufficiency of the evidence.
9. Analyze how two or more texts address similar themes or topics in order to build knowledge or to compare the approaches the authors take.

Range of Reading and Level of Text Complexity

    10. Read and comprehend complex literary and informational texts independently and proficiently.

(Common Core State Standards Initiative, 2012, p. 35)

Chapter Three

Writing for Real

A busy junior associate in an international law firm, attorney José Garcia spends his morning drafting a brief to be submitted to the court in advance of an upcoming trial. The brief requires significant technical language and precise wording to ensure that the judge understands both the legal argument and the legal precedents relevant to the facts of the current case.

Sara Woods, a nursing assistant in a busy metropolitan hospital, takes time to carefully document her work throughout the day. Maintaining clear, well-organized records of patient interactions, test results, and drug dosages is essential to ensuring that the patient care team is able to effectively interact and provide optimal medical services to the patients.

Long passionate about the environment, Brian Turner uses the skills he learned as a reporter for his college newspaper to report scientific findings for Greenpeace. Part advocate, part translator, Brian makes complex data accessible and meaningful for a general audience. He also shapes and reshapes the writing in press releases, annual reports, email blasts, and newsletters to target specific interests and appeal to particular audiences.

Stay-at-home mom Martha Green has turned her love of jewelry into a small business, designing and marketing handcrafted earrings and necklaces. In addition to teaching herself beading and metalworking, Martha has also had to learn how to write ad copy, prepare billing statements, and describe and sell her products over email and through social media. Martha finds that the powers of persuasion she uses in her jewelry business are also useful in her roles as her children's room mom at school and soccer mom—getting others to volunteer for bake sales and classroom projects requires a thoughtfully worded "sales pitch" too!

The Demand for Writing

The ability to write, and write effectively, is more important than ever. In *Because Writing Matters* by the National Writing Project and Carl Nagin (2006), the authors state, "Writing is a gateway for success in academia, the new workplace, and the global economy, as well as for our collective success as a participatory democracy" (p. 2). As the world becomes more technologically driven, it might be tempting to believe that writing is less of a priority. But in reality, the reverse is true. Certainly the traditional pen-and-paper forms of writing have faded, but as technology allows us to connect with people throughout our community and around the world in real time and asynchronously, writing becomes even more important to ensure that we effectively communicate our ideas through a range of media and to a variety of audiences. William Zinsser, author of the classic expository writing text *On Writing Well*, comments, "The new information age, for all its high tech gadgetry, is finally writing-based. Email, the internet, and the fax are all forms of writing, and writing is, finally, a craft with its own set of tools, which are words. Like all tools, they have to be used right" (2001, p. xi).

The accounts of José, Sara, Brian, and Martha demonstrate some of the varied forms and purposes of writing in the workplace. These four individuals represent a wide range of fields and career stages, but each is required to effectively use written language to communicate. A 2004 survey of 120 major American corporations found that in many workplaces writing is considered a "threshold skill" for both hiring and promotion (National Commission on Writing, 2004). With multiple candidates vying for entry-level positions, applicants are unlikely to be considered for an interview if they cannot effectively present themselves in writing. Employees looking for advancement must demonstrate that they can effectively communicate in writing in order to be trusted with promotion. Although once restricted to primarily managerial and professional positions, the need for effective writing and communication skills now extends to technical, clerical, and support positions as well and includes sectors ranging from manufacturing to construction, government, and the service industries (Alliance for Excellent Education, 2007). As one respondent to the 2004 survey noted, "Writing skills are fundamental in business. It's increasingly important to be able to convey content in a tight, logical, direct manner, particularly in a fast-paced technological environment" (NCW).

This demand for writing today is significantly different from that in previous generations. The Alliance for Excellent Education states, "The typical high school graduate of the 1870's, 1970's or even 1990's couldn't have dreamed of a world as saturated with writing as now exists" (2007, p. 1). UCLA's Mike Rose further notes that the stakes for learning to write have changed: "The benchmark for what counts as literate writing, what good writing requires, and how many people need to be literate in our society has moved dramatically" (1989, qtd. in NWP & Nagin, 2006, p. 2). And it isn't just the workplace that demands increased writing skill. Colleges, universities, and technical training programs require writing engagement. Family life and community participation increasingly depend on writing and social media, as evidenced by Martha's application of her marketing skills to her role as a parent volunteer coordinator. Likewise, civic engagement, from Brian's work as a Greenpeace activist to local petitions to Internet opinion blogs to the 2011 Twitter-fueled revolutions in the Middle East, demands written communication and collaboration.

Effective writing skills are important at all stages of life, from early childhood through professional career, and across all aspects of life experience. The ability to convey complex ideas and information in a clear, succinct manner and to communicate with varied audiences for a range of purposes is critical for success for individuals and our society as a whole (USDOE, NCES, 1998). Inadequate writing skills inhibit achievement in academic and professional realms, whereas proficient writing skills help drive the "engine of opportunity and economic growth" (National Commission on Writing, 2003).

Writing Achievement: What Our High School Graduates Can Do

So with the demand for writing so high, what do statistics tell us about the achievement of our recent high school graduates? Are they prepared to adequately respond to the increasingly complex writing demands of academia, the work world, and civil society? Unfortunately, the answer, for too many students, is "no."

Results of the National Assessment of Educational Progress (NAEP) writing assessment for 2011 showed only 27 percent of eighth- and eleventh-grade students scoring at or above proficient in their writing achievement. About 80 percent of grades 8 and 11 students scored basic or above, a decline from the previous scores of 88 percent and 82 percent respectively in 2007 (USDOE, NCES, 2012b). Among those high school graduates who do make it to college, instructors estimate that 50 percent are unprepared for college-level writing (Peter D. Hart Research Associates, Inc., & Public Opinion Strategies, 2005). At least 25 percent of new community college students are required to enroll in a remedial, non-credit-bearing writing class (USDOE, NCES, 2003). Eighty-one percent of employers describe recent high school graduates as "deficient in written communications" (Casner-Lotto & Benner, 2006).

Equally disturbing is the mismatch between what recent high school graduates *can* write and what they are *expected* to be able to write. Mike Rose notes that "many young people come to university able to summarize the events in a news story or write a personal response to a play . . . but they have considerable trouble with what has come to be called critical literacy: framing an argument or taking someone else's argument apart [and] synthesizing different points of view" (1989, p. 188, qtd. in NWP & Nagin, 2006, p. 2). High school graduates, even those who manage to score as proficient or higher in standardized tests, often struggle to communicate their ideas effectively in reports, memos, briefs, and other forms of communication that dominate professional and technical writing. This misalignment between school writing and out-of-school writing is part of the reason private companies now spend an estimated $3.1 billion each year teaching their employees to write (National Commission on Writing, 2003, 2004).

"School" Writing

So what does writing instruction look like in schools? Why do too many of our graduates require remediation at college and in the workplace and lack the critical literacy skills we know are so important for an informed citizenry? The short answer is that too little writing instruction takes place in schools and that the instruction that does occur is often poorly aligned with out-of-school writing realities. Studies by NAEP, the National Council of Teachers of English (NCTE), the American Association of School Administrators (AASA), and the National Academy of Education's Commission on Reading all concluded that K–12 students don't get enough opportunities to write. A 2006 study by Applebee and Langer found that two-thirds of students surveyed reported that their weekly writing assignments added up to less than an hour of work. This held across grade levels and content areas, including English. Nine percent of high school students reported doing virtually no writing at all.

Equally troubling, the in-school writing that does take place often bears little resemblance to the kinds of composition and response that are required in out-of-school writing—the kinds of writing that fill the days of José, Sara, Brian, and Martha. The writing we do in schools tends to be driven by test standards, or perhaps more accurately, our *perceptions* of testing expectations. Too frequently, too many of us feel pressured to meet those expectations and thus we diminish writing to fill-in-the blank, short answer responses, worksheets, text summaries, writing journal entries, and lists, hoping that these will build factual knowledge and help students recall information for the test (Graham, 2008). Surveys associated with the NAEP assessment found that two-thirds of the writing that occurs in schools is word-for-word copying in workbooks and that compositions of a paragraph or more in length are infrequent, even in high school.

Why so little writing? As a teacher, you probably know the answer to this better than anyone. Testing and test prep is one factor. Limited teacher training, overcrowded classes, and the time it takes to read and respond to student writing effectively are other drivers of our current practices (Hillocks, 2002; Applebee & Langer, 2006). But there is also the incorrect assumption that writing is merely the "flip side" of reading and that if students are able to read, they will also be able to write. Several decades of literacy research tell us, however, that while reading and writing are complementary, they do not necessarily go hand in hand and that students can be proficient readers while still struggling to master writing (Fitzgerald & Shanahan, 2000).

Additionally, many teachers, especially at the secondary level and especially across the disciplines, incorrectly assume that teaching writing is someone else's job—the elementary school teacher's or the English language arts teacher's. Recent research helps us understand why this is not true. First, we know that writing is complex and demands many opportunities across multiple and varied contexts for students to become proficient. Although a single teacher can have a strong impact on a student's writing development, "the Herculean efforts of a few are no match for the sustained and concerted efforts of an entire organization" (Graham, 2008). Students need a lot of practice, over many years, in multiple subject areas to gain the kind of proficiency that will allow them to successfully navigate the writing demands of college, career, and community (Graham & Perin, 2007). And second, we know that effective writing assignments in content area classes actually enhance, rather than take away from, content area learning. Perceiving the "all teachers are teachers of literacy" campaign as an attempt to replace discipline-based content with decontextualized reading and writing instruction, many content teachers have understandably resisted the integration of writing instruction into math, science, or history classes (O'Brien, Stewart, & Moje, 1995; Lattimer, 2010). However, there is considerable evidence that, given the right context, writing instruction can enhance student learning in content area classes (Bangert-Drowns, Hurley, & Wilkinson, 2004; Graham & Perin, 2007; Shanahan, 2004; Sperling & Freedman, 2001).

If we move away from fill-in-the-blank, drill-and-kill style writing assignments and toward assignments that require students to wrestle with ideas, clarify their thinking, synthesize information, and critique others' arguments and defend their own, students will gain both deeper understanding of content and writing skills that are useful in school and can be transferred to writing in out-of-school contexts. These are the kinds of writing required of José, Sara, Brian, and Martha in their professional, advocacy, and community work, and they need to be the kinds of writing that we increasingly require of our students across grade levels and content areas.

What can teachers—especially content area teachers—do to increase the amount of writing students do in their classes, to use writing to enhance students' knowledge of the content, and to create an environment of "writing for real"? In the examples that follow, you will see how teachers from social studies, literature, science, and math have added writing in thoughtful and discipline-specific ways.

Writing for Real in the High School Classroom: An Example

For nearly a decade now, Scott Blake's eleventh-grade students have been compiling oral history accounts of World War II. What started as an informal class presentation has grown into a library shelf full of published volumes. "Originally, I invited a World War II veteran in as a guest speaker for Veterans Day," Scott explained. "He told stories the whole period and the kids were mesmerized. They paid more attention during that hour than they had for the previous two months of regular history class. I realized that I needed to capitalize on the human resources around us and get kids actually doing history rather than just reading about history."

For Scott's students, "doing history" means interviewing, investigating, collaborating, critically thinking, and doing lots and lots of writing. Teams of students are charged with interviewing individuals who have historical memory of World War II. In addition to combat veterans, students interview women who were involved in the war effort on the home front, Japanese Americans who faced internment, and people who were children at the time but have vivid memories of the war's impact on their own lives. After being assigned an interview subject from a list of individuals Scott has compiled over the years, students research the topic or issue about which the interview subject is an expert in order to build the kind of background knowledge they will need to ask thoughtful questions during the face-to-face interviews. Students prepare for the interviews in class sessions during which Scott uses a fishbowl approach to model how to conduct interviews and students then have a chance to practice by interviewing one another. From these practice interviews students learn how to take careful notes, ask follow-up questions, and build rapport during their actual interviews.

Student teams are then expected to work together outside of class to complete their interviews. Parent volunteers, community members, and alums are recruited to help with transportation and logistics. Scott dips into a small travel budget donated by the PTA to help provide bus fare for students and to cover gas costs for those interview subjects who are able to come to campus. Organizing logistics, as you might expect, can be the most challenging component of this project, but over the years, Scott has found that he can put more and more of that responsibility onto students. "These students are high school juniors. They are sixteen and seventeen years old and they know how to get around town for jobs and their social life. I used to try to coordinate everything for them, but I've learned that most can, with a little support, step up and figure out the logistics themselves." In addition to taking some of the burden off of the teacher, having students figure out logistics helps them to learn critical skills such as setting up an interview, coordinating with a team, dressing professionally, and showing up on time.

Once interviews are complete, student teams gather back in the classroom to compare notes and determine how best to craft their interviews into oral histories. They compare their interview notes with the background information previously gathered from their research, develop new questions, and investigate further through additional research and reading. Teams compare findings across interviews to synthesize information and consider how different experiences can lead to different interpretations of events. They discuss how to effectively present an individual's story to an audience that may not have much prior knowledge of the events being described. And they make difficult decisions about what to do with information that the research books deem inaccurate or irrelevant but that the interview subject describes with detail and fervor.

Throughout the outlining, drafting, and revision process, Scott provides guidance and support through mini-lessons and writing conferences with the student teams. During mini-lessons, he strategically shares and responds to samples of student work, leads the class in an analysis of a mentor oral history text, or thinks aloud about his own writing process in order to teach structure, content, and style appropriate to the discipline. Through these lessons, the students gain immediately applicable skills and strategies while also coming to understand what makes historical writing, and in particular the writing of community history, different from writing in English or science, as well as different from the textbook style of writing that many initially envision when they think of history writing.

Scott follows up these whole-class mini-lessons with conferences that provide feedback and guidance to students as they puzzle through the specifics of their oral history. Some of these conferences take place face to face, but many also take place online through inserted comments and live chats on the Google Docs platform that students use to draft their histories. "I can be sitting on my sofa watching TV while also monitoring their writing at 7:00 on a Thursday night," Scott comments, acknowledging that his embrace of online writing has dramatically changed the way he interacts with his students' writing. "Each group shares their documents with each other and with me and then I can see who is contributing what and how the document is evolving. Where I used to read materials only when they were essentially 'done,' now I can see where they are going with their ideas and I can pop in a comment or start chatting with a group through the chat feature on Google Docs or via video through Google Hangouts to ask questions, provide feedback, and redirect them when necessary. I've found that I spend about the same amount of total time overall, but it is interspersed over the course of the project. This makes it more manageable for me (after all, who likes to read the stack of papers at the end?) and more meaningful for them since they get feedback in the moment instead of after they want to be done." (See Figure 3.1.)

Figure 3.1. Screenshots of an ebook template and a Google Doc in progress.

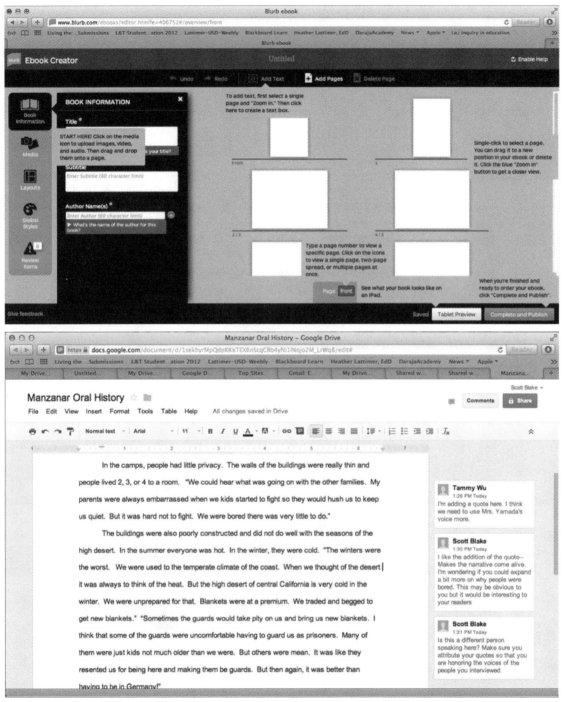

continued on next page

Figure 3.1. Continued.

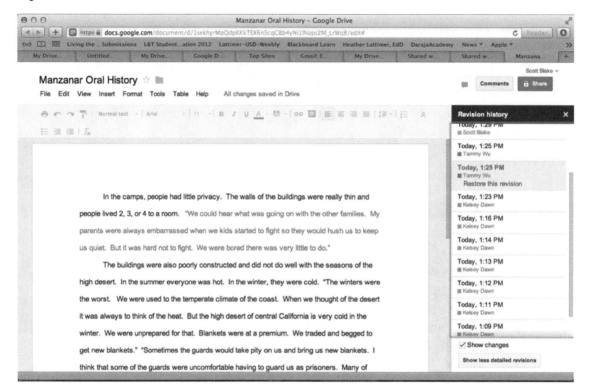

In the end, each bound and published volume the students produce features photos of the interview subjects, introductions and reflections by the research teams, and well-crafted narratives of individuals' lived experiences from World War II. The volumes are proudly displayed in the classroom and school library, and many students choose to purchase a copy to take home as well.[2] The publication of a real book with their names as authors is a thrill for most students, but for many the real highlight comes when they present a copy of the book to their interview subjects. "We've had many people cry when they receive the book," Scott explains. "They are so honored to think that their history matters enough to have it written down and published. It's a very emotional moment for everyone. Often the recipients will write letters after to tell us how proud they are, how they shared the book with their families, and sometimes it is the first time that their children or grandchildren heard the story. We've also received letters from family members after their relative passes, telling us how much they treasure the stories in the volume. Those letters are powerful. They show the kids that history matters and that their work matters." (See Figure 3.2.)

Figure 3.2. Letter from an interviewee.

Dear Jason, Tyler, Ana, and Mr. Blake,

It was such a joy to open and read the oral history book. I was honored to have my story included and touched to read the accounts by the other men and women who lived through World War II. I look forward to sharing the book with my grandchildren and hope that it will help them to understand a bit more of our shared past.

Sincerely -

Nathaniel Schwartz

Unpacking the Oral History Project: Characteristics of Writing for Real

Clearly, students in Scott's history class are engaged in the doing and writing of history. They approach their assignment in much the same way that adults in professional and civic life might approach a writing task and, in doing so, approximate the work of historians, journalists, and biographers. This approach increases student engagement, enhances historical understanding, and strengthens students' mastery of writing knowledge and skills. A close examination of what happens in Scott's classroom reveals the characteristics of real-world writing experiences listed in Figure 3.3.

Figure 3.3. Instructional strategies that support writing for real.

- **Discipline-Based Writing**
  - ◦ Engage students in writing that reflects the norms of the discipline.
  - ◦ Go beyond the use of writing-to-learn strategies.
- **Authentic Purpose and Audience**
  - ◦ Assign writing that responds to a real problem or seeks to answer an authentic question.
  - ◦ Have students share their writing with an audience of peers, professionals, and/or community members who will read and respond to their work.
- **Collaboration and Communication**
  - ◦ Provide opportunities for students to collaborate with peers at all stages of the writing and revision process.
  - ◦ Demonstrate the value of collaboration by holding students accountable for their contributions to the team.
- **Writing Is Thinking**
  - ◦ Provide flexibility in the structures and guidelines you give students so that they can adapt to meet the needs of their content and audience.
  - ◦ Deconstruct mentor texts with students so that they can recognize the structures and strategies authors used and then consider how to adapt them to their own writing.
- **Metacognition**
  - ◦ Encourage students to reflect on their learning process so that they can apply similar strategies when they are asked to write in other genres in the future.
- **Practice, Practice, Practice**
  - ◦ Provide multiple opportunities for students to write using a range of structures and forms that are appropriate to the discipline.
  - ◦ Give students time in class to write in order to demonstrate the value of writing and ensure that you are there to provide support when needed.

Discipline-Based Writing

The writing that students do in school needs to reflect the unique demands of specific disciplines. The writing of a scientist is distinct from the writing of a mathematician, engineer, novelist, or playwright. Writing in these disciplines demands distinct forms and unique ways of thinking. When we engage students in discipline-specific writing in our classrooms, we train them in the ways of thinking of the discipline (Hillocks, 1995).

> **Teaching Tip**
>
> Discipline-based writing assignments aren't limited to journal articles that academics write. Consider the kinds of writing employed by people who are in fields that use applied math, science, or humanities such as engineering, health sciences, or filmmaking. In each of these fields, writing can be used to inform, persuade, or entertain experts and novices alike. Varying the kinds of writing and types of audiences you are responding to in your classroom strengthens students' writing abilities and makes them more aware of potential applications and careers in your discipline.

In the oral history project, students in Scott's US history class have to grapple with the nature of primary sources, different perspectives, and apparent discrepancies between accounts. Uncovering varying stories leads to more questions, further research, and hard discussions about the nature of history as well as the nature of "truth." This history does not reflect the nice, tidy version of the past that is recounted in most US history textbooks. Instead, it's both messy and challenging. It pushes students out of their comfort zones and makes them reconsider what they thought they knew about other historical and contemporary events. It engages students in what Sam Wineburg terms *historical thinking*, teaching them to interrogate historical sources, form reasoned conclusions, and then communicate their best understanding of the past while recognizing that no account can ever fully represent historical events (2001). This approach approximates the work of academics and professional historians and teaches students the habits of mind appropriate to the discipline while also teaching the critical thinking and analysis skills that are required in many professions and needed in multiple aspects of civic life.

It is worth noting that engaging students in discipline-based writing goes beyond the writing-to-learn strategies often advocated by content literacy experts (see, for example, Fisher & Frey, 2007). Writing to learn describes the day-to-day writing activities that help students process, understand, and remember course material by prompting them to summarize, recall, question, or describe a lecture, video, reading, or activity in the classroom (Elbow, 1994). Strategies that fall within the writing-to-learn umbrella include exit slips, interactive notebooks, graphic organizers, learning logs, and reading journals. Such informal writing approaches have demonstrated value in helping students to process and retain content and provide formative assessment techniques that allow teachers to better evaluate what students do and do not understand (Knipper & Duggan, 2006).

Important as that approach can be, writing to learn does not help students develop discipline-based ways of thinking. Teaching the habits of mind of a historian, scientist, artist, or engineer requires that we engage students in writing experiences that go beyond summarizing information. There is a place for writing to learn, but students must also be asked to do the kind of writing that reflects the ways of thinking of the disciplines. They need to engage in writing that demands analysis, evaluation, interrogation, and synthesis of information; writing that puts forward and defends original arguments and ideas; writing that explores, postulates, and innovates. If we are to truly teach students in the disciplines, they must have opportunities to think and write in the ways of the disciplines.

Authentic Purpose and Audience

Real-world writing needs to have an authentic purpose and a real-world audience. I addressed the concept of authenticity in Chapter 1, but it is so important in writing instruction that it needs to be explored in greater depth here. Outside of school, people write to respond to genuine concerns and communicate with others in order to inform, persuade, enlighten, instruct, explain, or spur action. Rarely do individuals choose, on their own, to write without a clear purpose or audience, nor are they asked to do so by employers, who are wary of wasting time and resources. Linda Reif notes, "None of us wants to write for a meaningless exercise. Writing is hard work. We want our efforts to mean something; we want to know that our words made someone think, feel, or learn" (2007, p. 192).

In schools, however, we routinely ask students to engage in tasks with limited purpose or audience. Most assignments are read by an audience of one—the teacher. Such assignments require students to respond to a prompt that has limited purpose beyond the walls of the classroom: determining whether students did the reading, assessing if they can analyze the material, or teaching them to use the five-paragraph essay format. Students know that these assignments are limited in scope and utility and ask similarly limited questions in response: How long does it have to be? How will it be graded? Is this good enough? Too often, we've taken ownership of and interest in learning away from students. Too often, writing in schools isn't communication between a writer and an audience; it is a grade-driven transaction between a teacher and a student. As high school teacher and literacy expert Kelly Gallagher writes,

> Many of my students have come to think that there is only one audience—the teacher—and that writing is just another laborious school hoop to jump through. By the time they become seniors in high school the notion that audience might be someone other than their teacher has long since drowned in a decade long flood of "fake" writing—writing that they will never use outside of school. (2006, p. 130)

The oral history project in Scott's classroom provides students with an opportunity to write for an authentic purpose and a genuine audience. Students use their writing to communicate original accounts of past events, place those accounts

in a larger context, and reflect their own learning. They write these accounts for their interview
subjects, all of whom lived through a critical time
in our nation's past and most of whom have never
seen their story in print. Knowing that their stories
will be read by their interview subjects, individuals
whom the students come to respect and care about
over the course of the project, provides a powerful
incentive for students to take the writing seriously
and ensure both the integrity of the content and
the quality of the material. Scott reports that students work harder on this project than on almost

> **Teaching Tip**
>
> The audience for student writing doesn't have to take
> them outside the physical walls of the classroom.
> Posting to a class blog, writing letters to the editor, or
> even sharing work with peers within the classroom
> can all be considered forms of publishing student
> work. The venue can be flexible as long as students
> recognize the audience as authentic.

anything else they do during the year: "Even my struggling students, the kids who
you have to push to get to class on time, pay attention and do their homework. . . .
Even these kids are motivated by this project. They know it matters and they want
to do a good job."

Gallagher (2006) equates an authentic audience for a writer with the crowds
in the stands at a football game, noting, "Young writers also need 'Friday night
lights'—a place where they can show off their hard work" (p. 133). When Scott's
students unpack the boxes of bound and published books, when they share those
books with their families and friends, and, especially, when they present the books
to the individuals they interviewed, that is their "Friday night lights." Those moments may be less crowded and not as raucous as a Friday night at the football
stadium, but they can be just as meaningful for students. "I felt so proud when I
saw those books," one of Scott's students reported. "My name was on the cover
and my words were inside. I was a real author. I'd never imagined that I could be
an author before."

"The biggest thing for me," another student reported, "was when we gave
the book to Mrs. Rosenberg, the woman we interviewed. She didn't say a word at
first, just turned the pages, touching the pictures and the words with her gnarled-
up fingers. When she looked up at us she had tears in her eyes, and you could tell
how much it meant to her. It almost made me cry. I felt proud and humble all at
the same time. It was really cool." Engaging students in writing tasks that have
an authentic purpose and a real audience motivates and empowers. It provides
students with a sense of agency and a belief that they can use the written word to
accomplish goals and achieve something that is bigger than themselves (Doering, Beach, & O'Brien, 2007). Despite the dire warnings about the selfishness and
apathy of today's teens, most of the young people I've encountered care about the
world around them and want to make a difference. When we engage students in

authentic writing tasks for real purposes and genuine audiences, we provide them with the tools and the vision for how they might effectively use the written word to create change and contribute to the common good.

Collaboration and Communication

Although the image of the novelist tucked away in an isolated garret remains part of the popular conception of writing, most professional writers work in environments that are far from isolated. Look back at the examples at the beginning of this chapter. Attorney José Garcia will incorporate draft language from a team of paralegals into the brief he is crafting and, before he submits it to the judge, it will be reviewed and revised by a more senior attorney familiar with the case and knowledgeable about the habits and preferences of this particular judge. In Brian Turner's work at Greenpeace, he relies heavily on program scientists, borrowing and reshaping language from their original reports to make the information accessible for a general audience and then checking back with the scientists to ensure that he has accurately represented their findings. He also receives input from project coordinators and fundraisers who are more familiar with the target audience of each particular report, newsletter, or e-blast, often wandering down the hall to get suggestions about what has worked well in the past or simply to talk through ideas to make sure the message will resonate.

Interactive and collaborative processes fuel much of the writing that goes on outside of school. Interactions with peers, readers, reviewers, and supervisors help writers to clarify their thinking, communicate effectively, and ensure that they are achieving their intended purpose. But in school we often fail to provide opportunities for meaningful collaboration during the writing process. We might give our students time to brainstorm and pair-share ideas at the beginning of a writing assignment, but then students are often expected to go home and write on their own, a task that many adolescents find overwhelming. We may incorporate peer review opportunities before students submit their final drafts, but by this point few students want substantive feedback; they just want it to be "good enough" so they can turn it in and move on to the next task. The result of limiting collaboration in the classroom is that we limit both the quality of the thinking and the quality of the written product. To fully realize the potential of the writing process, at all stages we must provide meaningful opportunities to talk through ideas, get feedback, defend an approach, consider alternative

Teaching Tip

Holding students accountable for participation in collaborative teams is essential to avoid the frustration and inequity of "freeloading." Instructing students to document their contributions, monitoring the revision history in online tools such as Google Docs, observing collaboration in class, and requiring regular self- and peer assessments of participation and effort can help ensure that everyone is contributing to the work.

language, and integrate new learning.

In Scott's classroom, students have multiple opportunities for collaboration throughout the oral history project. They work in teams to research, plan, and conduct their interviews. They meet regularly as a whole class to share information and ideas across teams in order to learn from one another and explore different ways of approaching tasks and representing information. Within teams, they assign individual research and writing tasks but maintain constant communication to ensure that the final product will be a cohesive whole that will accurately represent both their interview subject and their research experience. Students are held accountable for both their individual contributions and their effectiveness as a member of a collaborative team. Reflecting on the project, one high-achieving student commented, "I was nervous when Mr. Blake first told us we would be working in teams. My grades matter a lot to me and I didn't want to be brought down by the group. But what I found was that I actually got better with my writing because of the input from my team members. I also learned that I have a tendency to take things over and that if I'm going to be a good team member I have to sometimes step back and listen."

In addition to strengthening the quality of the formal writing product, engaging students in a collaborative writing process also has the intended effect of providing them with multiple opportunities to practice less formal forms of written communication. Throughout the research, planning, drafting, revision, and publishing processes, students communicate with their team members through email, Twitter, and Facebook. They use Google Docs to write collaboratively, give feedback on drafts, and live chat with questions and comments on the process. Along the way, they pick up on communication norms ("When you put the email in all caps, it means you are shouting at me. Quit it!") and learn how to phrase feedback constructively ("Don't just tell me it's confusing, tell me what's confusing and what I should do to fix it."). They also develop greater comfort and facility with the written communication tools that dominate professional and civic life. "The textbooks talk about teaching students how to write a letter, and letters are important," Scott notes. "But day to day, these kids are going to use email, text messages, and other forms of online communication that haven't even been invented yet. Getting them to use online platforms now, to sometimes screw up on their netiquette and get called on it by their peers, will hopefully help prepare them to collaborate and communicate effectively in the future."

Writing Is Thinking

An effective real-world writing assignment has clear expectations but avoids giving so much structure that the writing becomes formulaic. It provides guidelines but still requires students to do the thinking work of shaping the content to make it

Teaching Tip

When students show you their writing and ask, "Is this OK?," strengthen their learning by turning the question back to them: "Is it effectively communicating your ideas?" "Does it respond to the needs and interests of your audience?" "Does it reflect the structures and language that we saw in the mentor texts?" Encouraging your students to assess their work for themselves enhances their understanding of discipline-based writing, builds confidence, and increases ownership.

meaningful to the intended audience for the intended purpose. In doing so, students are required to engage with material in a manner that deepens their understanding and lets them consider things they didn't know until they began to sort through the process of representing information and ideas in writing (Rief, 2007). Writing becomes an act of problem solving as students sort through the particulars of structure, word choice, format, and voice. It is a negotiation between information, ideas, audience, and purpose that builds knowledge of content and strengthens writing ability.

Leaders at the National Writing Project observe, "Many writers don't know their subject well until they've written a draft; few professional writers start with a topic sentence or outline; and most struggle through multiple drafts and acts of editing and revision" (NWP & Nagin, 2006, p. 25). Too often in classrooms, however, we reduce writing to a predigested outline structure, sometimes even providing students with suggested topic sentences, and then march them through a linear process of brainstorming, outlining, drafting, editing, through completion. This reduction is well intended; we want to simplify the writing to ensure that students are successful. However, in the simplification we take all of the thinking out of the process.

Real-world writing is challenging and messy. It requires multiple cognitive processes and rarely proceeds directly from one stage of the process to the next.

> Studies of how writers actually work show them shuffling through phases of planning, reflection, drafting and revision, though rarely in a linear fashion. Each phase requires problem solving and critical thinking. . . . Successful writers grasp the occasion, purpose, and audience for their work. They have learned how to juggle the expectations of diverse readers and the demands of distinct forms. (NWP & Nagin, 2006, p. 10)

If we want our students to be prepared to meet the demands of real-world writing, we need to give them the opportunity to approximate this work in the classroom, providing guidelines, models, and supports but allowing them to do the challenging and messy work of determining how best to represent their ideas to their audience.

Scott describes his approach to supporting student writing in the oral history project by referencing Goldilocks: "It is a balance. I don't want to give them too much structure or else I take all the ownership away. But I don't want to give them too little support because then they become overwhelmed. It has to be just right. And each year, and for each kid, that 'just right' may be a little different." The scaffolding Scott provides to everyone includes mentor texts of published oral history accounts by professional historians, sample oral histories written by the previous year's students, and a one-page set of guidelines for the project. He leads students through the process of deconstructing the mentor texts and considering how writers vary their structure and style in response to their purpose and audience. Scott also writes alongside the students, conducting his own oral history interview and sharing his own writing to model the art of problem solving as he talks through the choices he is making in structure, style, word choice, and revision. During the process, he regularly checks in with students, reading their drafts online, leaving comments on their Google Docs, meeting with individuals and small groups of students during in-class writing conferences, and answering questions sent via email or the class blog. Scott guides, mentors, and supports, but ultimately, the students make the decisions. They have to do the hard work of thinking because that is where the learning takes place.

Metacognition

The variety of forms of writing required in the world outside the classroom is nearly endless: reports, scripts, lists, accounts, records, emails, agreements, memos, articles, blogs, tweets, narratives, poems, schematics, graphs, manuals, charts, and on and on and on. And the possibilities increase every year as technology creates new communication platforms and social norms evolve in response to those platforms. It is impossible to teach our students how to compose every genre of text or structure of written communication. There is not enough time in the school day and, even if there were, we cannot anticipate the communication structures that will be expected in two, five, or ten years when our students enter the worlds of professional and civic life and leadership. Therefore, it is imperative that we equip students with ways of noticing and thinking about texts that will empower them to understand and learn how to use a range of forms of writing in the future.

In his book *Time for Meaning*, Randy Bomer draws a parallel between teaching writing and his occasional pursuit of woodworking. He explains that most days he pays little attention to the way that joints are put together or to the grains of wood on a plank floor, but when he is involved in a project of his own, he suddenly notices more. As an avid hobbyist, he has learned to pay attention to models of woodworking that can help him become more proficient at the craft. We need to teach our students to develop similar metacognitive habits around writing, Bomer asserts:

> Helping students learn how to learn about different genres of writing empowers
> them to find a way of writing that counts in the different communities they will move
> through in their lives. I don't teach poetry so that kids will remember all about writing

Teaching Tip

Reserving the last four to five minutes of the class period to check in on progress can be immensely helpful for both students and teacher. Use informal discussion or exit slips to get students to reflect on prompts such as the following:

- What did you learn today?
- What are you finding challenging?
- How can you overcome this challenge?
- What supports do you need to be successful?

Recognizing progress and thinking through challenges helps students to become independent and self-aware problem solvers and lets teachers know when and how to step in to assist students with whole-class instruction or targeted individual or small-group support.

poems and be able to do it forever. I want them to develop habits of mind related to learning a genre, so that they can learn in whatever genres they need. (1995, p. 119)

During the oral history project unit, Scott regularly asks his students to step back from the immediacy of the work they are doing to reflect on their writing process and their writing choices: What did you learn from this mentor text? What do you still need to learn? Where could you find other mentor texts? How did you adapt your writing to respond to your audience? How might you write differently if you were writing for a different audience? What was most helpful about working with a collaborative team? How did you overcome frustrations? What did you learn about yourself as a writer? What are your strengths? What do you want to improve and how could you work on making that improvement? Pausing to consider these questions helps students to recognize the craft of writing and to develop the habits of mind that will be needed across genres and writing experiences.

Practice, Practice, Practice

Writing is complex. Becoming an effective writer is not something that can be accomplished through one writing task, no matter how authentic the experience. The road from novice to expert requires multiple opportunities to practice writing for many different audiences and purposes across a range of genres and content areas. Although writing is hard and teaching it can be challenging, there is no substitute for getting involved in the messy process of writing. We learn to write by writing (Rief, 2007). In a 2008 report summarizing the research literature on effective instructional strategies for supporting the development of competent adolescent writers, the number one conclusion was that teachers need to regularly dedicate classroom time for sustained real-world writing opportunities (Graham, 2008). Surveys of students who had taken the NAEP test at grades 8 and 12 found that those who were engaged at least twice a month in sustained writing tasks that included planning and revising outperformed their peers who had fewer opportunities to write in class (NWP & Nagin, 2006).

Students in Scott's US history class complete only one oral history project each year, but this is certainly not the only time they engage in complex writing tasks. Early in the year, they design and curate museum displays about the drafting of the Constitution and its impact on the world today. During the unit on the Civil War and Reconstruction, they research, script, and film mini-documentaries. And at the end of the year, they create an online newsmagazine detailing contemporary concerns and describing their historical roots. Many students report that they write more in Scott's class than they do in some of their English classes. Scott acknowledges that this approach to history teaching is more work than the lectures and multiple-choice tests favored by some of his colleagues, but he firmly believes that it is worth the effort:

> **Teaching Tip**
>
> More writing doesn't necessarily mean more papers. Defined broadly, writing can also take the form of films, displays, infographics, blogs, and multimodal compositions. As long as the text is authentic to the discipline and involves students synthesizing information and ideas to communicate their understanding for an audience, many genres can "count" as writing.

> The writing that we do helps my students to become better historians, better thinkers, and better people. They consistently outperform their peers on standardized history tests. They come back from college and report that they are better prepared to do the work in their history and social science courses. I hear them in the hallways having thoughtful conversations about current events and global concerns. And they are more confident in their ability to assert themselves and communicate their ideas.

If our job as teachers is about more than a simple transfer of knowledge, if our job is truly about empowering a generation of young people, then engaging them in authentic, discipline-based writing is essential.

Classroom Portraits of Real-World Writing

In the following sections, you will find classroom portraits of real-world writing from a range of classrooms, grade levels, and content areas. They reflect quite different approaches to the challenge of creating authentic writing and learning experiences that are responsive to the demands of the discipline. All of them, however, have elements of the characteristics described in Figure 3.3 and in the discussion of Scott's oral history project. As you read, consider how each of the characteristics works within the example profiled. And then you might want to think about how you could apply these characteristics and the questions in the following list to writing assignments in your own classroom. What are you already doing to support writing in this way? What could you add to your own repertoire that would strengthen disciplinary writing?

- **Discipline-Based Writing.** How does the assignment engage students in discipline-based ways of thinking?
- **Authentic Purpose and Audience.** Is there a real purpose for doing this work? Who is the audience?
- **Collaboration and Communication.** Are students participating in a collaborative writing community? Is the assignment helping to develop informal written communication skills?
- **Writing Is Thinking.** What is the balance between structure and ownership? Are students engaged in the thinking work of crafting text that is responsive to the content as well as to their purpose and audience?
- **Metacognition.** Are there opportunities for students to consider the process of writing and to reflect on their own learning?
- **Practice, Practice, Practice.** Do students have regular opportunities to engage in authentic writing experiences within this classroom as well as across content areas and grade levels?

Theme-Driven Picture Books

Throughout the required *To Kill a Mockingbird* unit in Diana Newell's ninth-grade English classroom, the students engage in rich conversations about the concepts of justice, race, class, and morality. They debate the courtroom drama, create character profiles to attempt to understand varying perspectives, and eagerly follow Scout's evolution as she grows and matures in response to events in the world around her. At the end of the unit, in most of Diana's colleagues' classrooms, students are required to write the traditional response to literature analysis essay. When she first started teaching, Diana required this essay too, but she found that it often fell flat. "It was like we had all this enthusiasm and excitement at the end of the book, and then we assigned the essay and the kids totally deflated. That writing assignment almost completely erased whatever interest they had had in the book."

For the past several years, Diana has taken a new tack. Students still write informal analytical responses in preparation for class discussions, but at the end of the unit, instead of a formal essay, they create picture books. The picture books build on one of the themes in the novel but ask students to go beyond the particular characters and events in the novel itself to create a story that is relevant and responsive to contemporary manifestations of these themes. The picture books students create are published and presented to children at a local elementary school.

Diana reports that the success of the project has exceeded her original expectations: "Initially I just thought it was a fun way to explore themes from the novel. But what I've found is that this assignment engages students in a much deeper analysis of *Mockingbird*." Guided by their teacher, students revisit the novel to examine how Harper Lee develops themes, the techniques she employs to build character, and her use of dialogue, perspective, and language. They then determine how to employ these techniques in their own stories, adapting the novelist's strategies to fit their purpose and audience (see Figures 3.4 and 3.5 for a sample storyboard and a page from a student book). "Because the students are actually using the techniques in their own stories, rather than just reporting on the techniques in an essay for their teacher, I've found they pay a lot more attention. They have Post-its all over their copies of the novel and constantly refer back to the novel while they are working on their own books."

To ensure that students are able to articulate their thinking (and to allay the fears of her colleagues), Diana requires her students to craft an Author's Note to include inside the front cover of each picture book. In these notes, students explain the thematic connections with *Mockingbird*, discuss the stylistic influences of the novel, and describe the rationale behind their choices as authors. "Some of these

Figure 3.4. Sample storyboard.

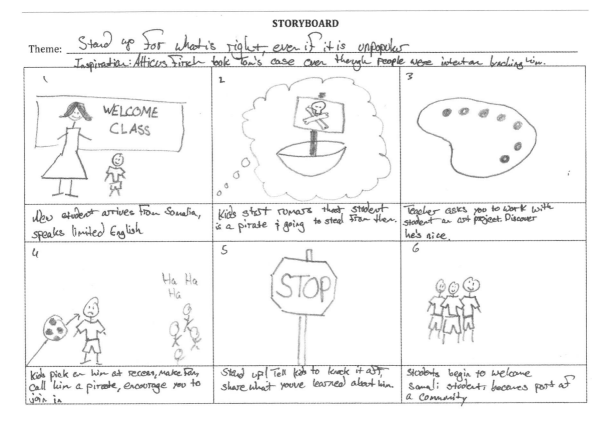

Figure 3.5. Sample page from a student picture book.

Madar stood quietly while the other kids taunted him.
    "Can't speak English."
    "Must be a pirate."
    "Aren't all Somalis pirates?"
    "Watch out! He'll steal your stuff."
    "Arrgh!"

Kyle could see the tears welling in Madar's eyes. He wanted to step in to help Madar. But something held him back. Kyle worried that if he intervened then some of the kids might turn on him. They might stop being his friend or call him names. Already there were rumors that he was a "pirate lover."

One of the kids kicked the soccer ball hard in Madar's direction. This wasn't a friendly kick. This was aimed at Madar's head. It was intended to hurt.

Enough! "Stop," Kyle yelled, **"STOP!!"**

notes end up being longer than the analytical essays that their peers are writing in other classes. And almost all of them are more thoughtful," Diana comments with a wry smile. "The students are really proud of their work. They love presentation day when we take the books over to the elementary school and read them to the fourth and fifth graders. They are delighted to see their name in print and to have their books in the library. They want to preserve their thinking, 'for posterity,' as one student told me. When they write their author's note, it is their chance to demonstrate their knowledge and show off all of the smart author decisions they made."

Diana still hears some grumbling from other teachers at her school. Many of their concerns have been alleviated, however, because these picture book authors have moved into grades 10, 11, and 12 with analytical skills that are just as strong, if not stronger, than those of their peers. A recent visit from Department of Literature faculty at a local university further supported Diana's approach when the university faculty reported that they often spend the first year unteaching the five-paragraph essay in favor of more flexible approaches that better respond to the writer's voice and intent. But the most important response has come from Diana's students: "I survey the students at the end of the year and every year, the picture book project rates number one as the 'favorite assignment' and 'assignment where I learned the most,'" Diana reports. "I've had former students tell me they were taking their book with them to college. A few of my colleagues have started doing the project just because they get pressure from the students. It's been amazing to see what started off as a fairly off-the-cuff idea blossom into something that has been motivating and meaningful for my students. It has shaped their identity as readers and writers of literature."

Science Research Proposals

In Alexa Ramos's chemistry class, the concept of a high school research proposal has been turned on its head. Rather than simply have students go through the traditional steps of writing out a research question and hypothesis for a cookie-cutter science fair project that is heavily teacher directed, Alexa expects her students to build on the knowledge they gain through classroom study and lab-based inquiry activities to create an original research proposal that has the potential to contribute to the field of study. Alexa, who spent several years doing postbaccalaureate research work in a university chemistry lab, explained that the impetus for engaging students in this project came from her own experience in the field: "At the university, the research proposal is where a lot of the thinking takes place. Researchers have to know their field well, be up-to-date on the latest scientific findings, and then ask an original question or propose an innovative approach." She notes that the stakes are high and that proposal authors need to be very aware of their purpose and audience: "If you don't do a good job on your proposal, you don't get funding, and most labs, both in the university and in the private sector, are heavily dependent on grant funding."

Throughout the early months of the school year, Alexa asks students to begin to think and write like scientists. After each unit and every lab activity, she requires students to brainstorm questions that were prompted by the learning: What questions does this unit raise? What else do you want to know? How do the concepts in this unit connect with science-related challenges we encounter in the world today?

At first, the questions students ask are stilted and formulaic, but over time they begin to generate original questions that demonstrate they are starting to think like scientists: Is it possible to have a superconductor at room temperature? How far can elements on the periodic table extend? How can electromagnetic energy be efficiently converted into chemical energy?

By the beginning of the second semester, students have a collection of research ideas in their science notebooks. They've acquired a solid foundation of content knowledge and begun to approximate ways of thinking appropriate to the discipline. Alexa then presents them with their research challenge. Working in teams, students develop research proposals, complete with an original question, literature review, proposed methodology, and description of potential implications. They can draw on one of the ideas they generated during the previous semester or develop a new idea. Each proposal is submitted to a review board made up of other teachers, a university professor, and several members of the local scientific community. The strongest proposals are awarded funding using donations from the PTA and a small education grant from a local biotech company.

The idea of putting together a real research proposal that will be reviewed by actual scientists is at first daunting for many students. But Alexa gives them plenty of models, lots of support, regular access to expert mentors, and, for inspiration, presentations by recent graduates. "I know it seems scary," one former student commented, "but when you put it together, it is actually really cool. Doing this work made me realize that chemistry isn't just something in a textbook; it can have a real-world impact." Many of Alexa's students have gone on to study science in college, and several have been offered internships in local labs while still in high school.

And, Alexa reflects, even for those who don't end up studying science or working in the scientific community professionally, the knowledge they gain by being asked to generate a research proposal is invaluable: "I want each of my students to understand that scientific understanding continues to evolve, but it evolves through systematic research and rigorous scrutiny within the scientific community. This understanding is essential if they are to be informed citizens and consumers." Being asked to craft a research proposal that mirrors the writing of professional scientists takes students deeper into the content and helps them understand the ways of thinking in the discipline while also strengthening critical thinking skills and writing strategies that can be used across disciplines and professional and civic contexts.

Online Algebra Problem Solving

Not all authentic audiences need to be outside of the classroom. In Marc Salazar's algebra class, students have been piloting a one-to-one laptop adoption for the past several years that allows them to take home the computers, and a special grant provides at-home Internet access. With this setup, Marc can extend learning beyond the school day through online social networking. As part of students' regular homework, Marc posts problems to solve on Edmodo, a Facebook-like platform designed for schools. As students work to solve the problems, they reach out to their peers to check their work, ask questions, make suggestions, and consider alternative approaches. Recent online conversations featured posts like those found in Figure 3.6.

Marc observes that at first students have to be required to post their comments to the site, but within a few weeks they are readily engaging in the written conversation.

> Students like it because they feel like they aren't alone when they are working on the problems. And I like it because it means that they are learning to rely on one another and learn from each other. My favorite moments are when there are several different kids on the site and it's almost like they are having a written argument about how to solve the problem. I jump online and there is this transcript of energized algebraic thinking. How often can you get a bunch of teenagers to write passionately about math?

The written dialogue that Marc's students are engaged in mirrors the work of professional discourse among mathematicians, physicists, engineers, statisticians, game developers, computer programmers and others who problem-solve through a collaborative approach that is increasingly global as facilitated by online conversation. As students write, they learn to represent their thinking through discipline-appropriate literacy practices, they deepen their understanding of the concept under exploration, and they strengthen their understanding of what mathematics is all about. "They are just coming to understand that math isn't about formulas," Marc explains. "It's about logic, inquiry, and justifying your thinking. I've had students who come into this class saying, 'Why do I have to learn this?' leave thinking that they want to study math or engineering in college. That's pretty cool!"

Figure 3.6. Student posts on an algebra problem.

Randy B. to **Advanced Algebra 2012-2013**

I have a theory for n/0. I know we were all taught that it is impossible to do such an equation, but (since we were all little kids in kindergarten) we were all taught that division is repeated subtraction. So if you were to take 0 away from any number it would be infinite. Look at it this way you have n oranges no matter what no matter how many times you give away 0 oranges will you ever reach 0, this means that n/0 = infinity. If there is a problem in my theory please let me know but I'm pretty confident it is correct if you look at it as repeated subtraction, which division is.

Show Less

Jan 23, 2013

 Alexis D. - Um I don't really get it. + n/0=0 not infinite
Jan 23, 2013

 Jorge M. - Technically, division is splitting a number in to a certain amount of groups. So, if we put "n" into zero groups, we get nothing because there are no groups.
Jan 24, 2013

 Randy B. - 6/1 how many times can you take away 1, 6 times.
Yesterday

 Randy B. - 6/2 how many times can you take away 2, 3 times.
Yesterday

 Randy B. - 6/3 how many times can you take away 3, 2 times.
Yesterday

 Randy B. - 6/0 how many times can you take away zero, infinite times because no matter how many times you take away nothing it will stay the same and you will never get 0.
Yesterday

Connection to the Common Core State Standards

The instructional guidelines illustrated in this chapter closely align with the writing expectations articulated in the Common Core State Standards (CCSS). Like the CCSS, the teachers and classrooms profiled here are dedicated to ensuring that students are prepared for the writing expectations of college, career, and civic engagement when they graduate from high school. If students are engaged in crafting texts authentic to their discipline, for example, they must learn to use valid reasoning, substantiate their ideas with evidence, and convey complex ideas that are representative of the kinds of historical, scientific, mathematical, and/or literary analyses found in their fields (see standards 1 and 2). Learning to do this kind of writing within and across disciplines requires that students learn to adapt their writing structures, styles, and approaches to their purpose and audience (see standards 4 and 10). Designing discipline-based writing experiences that routinely engage students in responding to authentic purposes and audiences through a collaborative, metacognitive process directly supports the skills and understandings required by the CCSS.

College and Career Readiness Anchor Standards for Writing, Grades 6–12

Text Types and Purposes

1. Write arguments to support claims in an analysis of substantive topics or texts using valid reasoning and relevant and sufficient evidence.
2. Write informative/explanatory texts to examine and convey complex ideas and information clearly and accurately through the effective selection, organization, and analysis of content.
3. Write narratives to develop real or imagined experiences or events using effective technique, well-chosen details, and well-structured event sequences.

Production and Distribution of Writing

4. Produce clear and coherent writing in which the development, organization, and style are appropriate to task, purpose, and audience.
5. Develop and strengthen writing as needed by planning, revising, editing, rewriting, or trying a new approach.
6. Use technology, including the Internet, to produce and publish writing and to interact and collaborate with others.

Research to Build and Present Knowledge

7. Conduct short as well as more sustained research projects based on focused questions, demonstrating understanding of the subject under investigation.
8. Gather relevant information from multiple print and digital sources, assess the credibility and accuracy of each source, and integrate the information while avoiding plagiarism.
9. Draw evidence from literary or informational texts to support analysis, reflection, and research.

Range of Writing

10. Write routinely over extended time frames (time for research, reflection, and revision) and shorter time frames (a single sitting or a day or two) for a range of tasks, purposes, and audiences.

(Common Core State Standards Initiative, 2010, p. 41)

Chapter Four

Authentic Listening and Speaking

Programmer Chris Adams has spent the past several months working on algorithms that demonstrate the effects of wind on the characters and objects in a video game soon to be released by the software company where he works. To ensure that his work will fit with the code being written on characters, background, and story line, Chris is constantly collaborating with his colleagues. Collaboration includes everything from daily meetings, in which team members provide progress checks and demo their work for feedback, to the informal bull pen conversations, during which team members share ideas, offer advice, and problem-solve together.

Amanda Scott feels as though she spends most of each day honing her oral communication skills. A member of the wait staff at an upscale restaurant, Amanda uses her presentation skills at each table as she describes the day's specials, makes suggestions about wine pairings, and tempts patrons with dessert. Listening is critical too. She not only needs to get patrons' orders right, but she also needs to be able to understand and be responsive to food allergies, dietary restrictions, and individual preferences. Good listening paired with an engaging presentation is key to healthy tips.

A financial analyst in a large multinational corporation, James Le has had to become skilled at presenting complex data to a variety of audiences using a range of media. From PowerPoint presentations for board members to Web seminars for shareholders, James has learned that a successful presentation demands both clear graphics that distill the data and strong oral communication skills that help him to tailor the information in the moment based on audience feedback.

Church pastor and community leader Coretta Williams tells her friends that getting up and speaking from the pulpit on Sunday mornings is the easy part of her job; it's facilitating communication between parishioners that presents challenges. More than twenty-plus years as a choir member, Sunday school coordinator, mother of five grown children, and most recently ordained minister have taught Coretta how to listen, ask thoughtful questions, and communicate responses in a manner that builds consensus and prioritizes the well-being of the community. These same communication skills have empowered Coretta to advocate for her church and community, most recently as leader of a successful campaign to shut down several bars in the area that were repeat offenders in selling alcohol to minors.

The Need for Effective Oral Communication

The diverse experiences of Chris, Amanda, James, and Coretta illustrate the range of speaking and listening skills that are necessary today. To effectively engage in the workplace, higher education, and community and civic life, individuals need to be proficient in many forms of both formal and informal oral communication. They need to be able to speak and listen effectively in diverse contexts, including one-on-one conversations, small-group collaborations, large-scale presentations, and virtual communication through video conferences, Web seminars, and live chats.

The Partnership for 21st Century Skills (P21), a research and advocacy organization of leading business and education organizations, lists communication as one of their "4Cs," essential learning and innovation skills required for success in college, career, and civic life. Their description of vital communication skills includes a person's ability to articulate thoughts and ideas clearly, to listen carefully to decipher meaning, to communicate orally for a range of purposes, and to effectively use a range of media in diverse environments (P21, 2011). The National Association of Colleges and Employers, in their 2012 survey of 244 employers, ranked oral communication as the most important skill or quality of prospective job candidates. On a five-point scale, survey respondents scored the "ability to verbally communicate with persons inside and outside of the organization" as 4.63 on average, significantly higher than elements that we traditionally think of as in demand, such as technical knowledge (3.99) or computer proficiency (3.95) (NACE, 2012).

Some of us, of course, recognize what at first seems to be a paradox in these statistics: at a time when digital media and virtual communication platforms are rapidly expanding, the demand for effective oral communication skills is greater than ever. However, when you think about it, it's precisely because there are more diverse ways of communicating and more diverse audiences with whom we can communicate that effective oral communication skills are increasingly essential. When financial analyst James Le interacts with shareholders from around the world, he needs to be very aware of cultural and linguistic differences as well as technology challenges that might cause miscommunication. Similarly, when pastor Coretta Williams connects with parishioners, many of whom come to her with sensitive issues and sometimes widely divergent views, her awareness of language, tone, and body language help to ensure that she is effectively understanding their concerns and communicating her responses. And we know that the potential benefits of effective communication can be great and that the costs of miscommunication can be steep, both individually and organizationally, as measured by gratuities collected, programming deadlines met, community trust, or stock price fluctuations.

Effective oral communication is also critical to getting hired and advancing in your career. Employment consultant J. P. Hansen observes, "It is not always the best person on paper who lands the job. . . . [T]he ability to verbalize clear, concise answers is paramount'" (qtd. in Driscoll, 2011). Career expert Lindsey Pollak agrees, noting that even in technical fields, oral communication skills are essential to career advancement: "'It's so rare to find somebody who has that combination of really good technical skills and really good verbal communication skills. . . . You will be head and shoulders above your colleagues if you can combine those two'" (qtd. in Driscoll, 2011).

At the college and university level, effective oral communication skills in the classroom support students' content learning success as they participate in discussions, listen to live or virtual lectures, and collaborate with peers on group projects or labs. Additionally, confidence in oral communication is a key determinant in helping students, particularly students from underrepresented backgrounds, to successfully navigate through to degree completion (Tough, 2012). Students who are confident in their speaking and listening abilities are more likely to ask questions in class, admit confusion, attend office hours, and ask for help from faculty and peers than those who are less confident in their oral communication skills. This willingness to seek out support and advocate for their own success is critical, especially since more than one-third of American students who start college will fail to finish in six years—the highest college dropout rate in the industrialized world (USDOE, NCES, 2012a).

This need for clear communication skills is evident in our civic and community life as well. At a time when political divisiveness appears increasingly rampant, the ability to engage in thoughtful oral discourse is more important than ever. As a society, we need listeners who seek to hear and understand a diversity of viewpoints. And we need speakers who use their voices both to articulate their own views and to engage in collaborative dialogue to find consensus. These listeners and speakers may be politicians, policymakers, and community leaders like Coretta Williams, the church pastor, who are professionally engaged in civic discourse, but they can also be ordinary citizens who advocate for a cause, participate in discussions around school and community development, or simply work to improve communication around contentious issues over conversations around the water cooler. Schools play a critical role in developing both the skills and the dispositions needed for effective civic and community discourse. Amy Gutmann writes, "Schools have a much greater capacity than parents and most voluntary organizations for teaching children to reason out loud about disagreements that arise in democratic politics" (1999, p. 4). This greater capacity arises from the reality that students in schools are more likely to encounter a diversity of experiences and viewpoints than they will find in their homes, places of worship, or special interest organizations (Gutmann, 1999; Parker, 2003).

Teaching students to engage in thoughtful dialogue in schools equips them to participate in meaningful discussions later in life and increases the likelihood that they will choose to do so. A study of 90,000 students in twenty-eight countries found that classroom discussion of controversial issues in an open classroom environment was a significant predictor of civic knowledge, support for democratic values, participation in political discussion, and political engagement (Torney-Purta, Lehmann, Oswald, & Schulz, 2001). A 2003 study in this country found that participating in meaningful discussions in school increased the likelihood that young adults would actively participate in civic activities after they left school (Andolina, Jenkins, Zukin, & Keeter). Additionally, evidence suggests not only that these students are more likely to participate but also that they are more likely to be oriented toward tolerance, problem solving, and consensus building in their participation (Avery, 2002).

Listening and Speaking Competency: What Our High School Graduates Can Do

With the high demand for strong oral communication skills in the professional arena, higher education, and our communities, how do our high school graduates measure up? Are they able to demonstrate the necessary listening and speaking competencies?

Results are mixed. On the one hand, high school graduates have had more practice in aspects of their oral communication skills than in the other literacy competencies of reading and writing. After all, most have been listening and speaking since infancy. However, the register of oral communication practiced in social conversation is typically quite different from that expected in professional or academic discourse. Career expert Lindsey Pollak advises prospective job applicants, "'You've been talking your whole life, but not in this way. . . . There's so much focus on e-mail and instant messaging texting . . . that I think we've lost a little bit of that ability to talk in a professional way'" (qtd. in Driscoll, 2011). Both prospective employers and college instructors bemoan what is often perceived as an erosion of professional discourse. "Um," "like," "whatever," and, my personal pet peeve, "ya know" are examples of casual modes of communication that have crept into contexts where more formal registers have traditionally been the norm.

On the 2012 National Association of Colleges and Employers survey, employers graded their average new recruits at a B+ in verbal communication skills. This score was higher than that for written communication but lower than the grade for teamwork skills. A 2005 survey of 400 employers and 1,487 recent high school graduates found that 46 percent felt there were gaps in students' preparation in oral communication and public speaking, with 15 percent reporting "large gaps" (Peter D. Hart Research Associates/Public Opinion Strategies, 2005). Thirty-four percent of respondents further reported dissatisfaction with the job that high schools were doing to prepare students in oral communication, a dissatisfaction rate that, while significant, was less than that for other core literacy areas, including preparing graduates to read and understand complex materials (41 percent).

"School" Communication

As any teacher knows, a number of impediments, or perceived impediments, seem to stand in the way of further developing students' listening and speaking skills in school. The first, and most obvious, is class size. With state and district budgets strained, class sizes have been pushed into the thirties and forties in many academic subjects. Having so many students in the room challenges the dynamics of holding whole-class discussions or requiring individual in-class presentations. Small-group discussions are also challenging since crowded classrooms may lack the physical space to allow for effective collaborative grouping.

Additional impediments derive from both internal concerns and external pressures. As with engaging students in meaningful reading and writing tasks, the pressure to "cover" content in preparation for high-stakes tests can trump opportunities to engage students in thoughtful discourse; even when students want to dig deeper and discuss a concept, there is pressure to move on to the next topic. Additionally, with schools under the political microscope, some teachers self-censor to avoid controversy, preferring to remain neutral and avoid topics that might cause tensions or risk bringing censure from parents and the community (Hess, 2004; Simon, 2001).

Despite these impediments, many teachers have found effective approaches to engaging students in meaningful and authentic listening and speaking in the high school classroom. Doing so helps prepare students for the world beyond high school and also strengthens their content knowledge and skills. Speaking and listening as they learn content allows students to try on new academic vocabulary, ask and respond to questions relevant to the focus topic, and develop communication strategies that are responsive to the discourse patterns of the discipline. As you read about Sheila Clark's math class in the pages that follow, notice how her well-crafted instruction strengthens both oral communication skills and students' content knowledge.

Authentic Listening and Speaking in the Secondary School Classroom: An Example

Visitors to Sheila Clark's ninth-grade algebra class typically find students clustered around a table fiercely debating math problems. Today's problem focuses on determining the ideal size of cookie cutter to use in a bakery. It is a deceptively simple problem because it requires a thoughtful understanding of algebraic functions, basic geometry, and strong mathematical reasoning to solve.

> A bakery machine creates a continuous stream of cookie dough that is 12 inches in width and ¼-inch thick. Cookies are cut from the dough using round cookie cutters that are pressed into the dough in rows, as shown below. The dough that is not used in the round cookies gets put into the waste pile. What diameter of cookie cutter will result in the least waste?

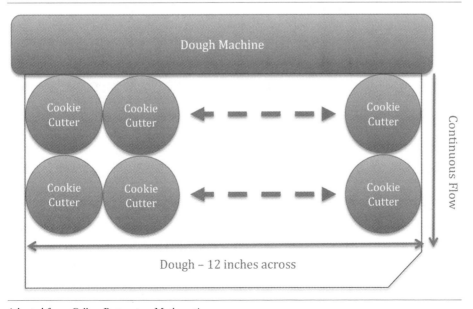

Adapted from *College Preparatory Mathematics.*

Problem solving in Sheila's class follows a clear protocol, one that involves reading, writing, speaking, and listening. Students begin by reading through the problem and asking their teacher questions to clarify their understanding of the question. They then spend several minutes working the problem on their own; Sheila encourages them to sketch out their thinking using images, mathematical symbols, and/or written notes. Students then cluster in teams of four to discuss the problem—initially taking turns to share their individual thinking and then working together to consider different problem-solving approaches, resolve any differences, and determine an appropriate solution. Conversation in one of today's teams included the following:

Taylor: I don't understand how to determine the volume, because there isn't a clear length.

Miguel: I don't think we have to do volume. We can just do area because the thickness is always a ¼ -inch and that isn't going to change no matter what size the cookie cutter.

Taylor: Okay, but even if we are finding area instead of volume, how do you know how long the dough is?

Shanice: I don't think it really matters how long it is, because each of the rows of cookie cutters is right next to the other, so we could decide to just figure out the area for one row of cookies.

Adrian: I like that. It makes sense because the size of the little diamonds in between the cookies is going to be the same regardless of the number of rows of cookies, so let's just figure it out for one [see Figure 4.1].

Miguel: Could we make it even simpler? Could we just figure it out for one cookie? What if we just look at the difference between the area of the circle and the area of the square with sides that are equal to the circle's diameter [see Figure 4.2]?

Adrian: That seems way too basic. There are going to be different numbers of diamonds depending on how many cookies can fit in the 12-inch sheet. If you had 2-inch cookies, then you'd have five diamonds in the middle, but if you have 4-inch cookies then you'll have only two diamonds.

Shanice: And what about if the cookie cutter is 5 or 7 inches in diameter or some other number that doesn't go into twelve evenly? Then there's even more extra dough at the end of the row. I think we have to consider the full row of cookies, not just one cookie.

Miguel: All right. I see your point.

Taylor: Wait. I still don't understand why we can just look at one row. If we do, then we aren't looking at the same area size in the original sheet and therefore we won't be able to compare amounts of waste. Don't we have to start with the same original sheet size for all of the cookie cutters?

Figure 4.1. Student drawing of a row of cookie cutters to solve a math problem.

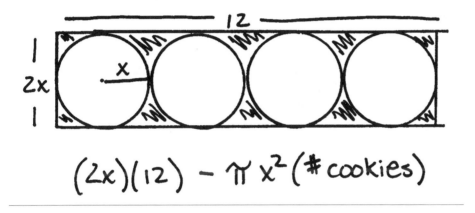

$$(2x)(12) - \pi x^2 (\# \text{cookies})$$

Figure 4.2. Student drawing of one cookie cutter to solve the math problem.

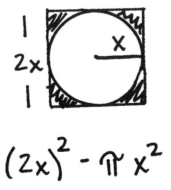

$$(2x)^2 - \pi x^2$$

Taylor's question prompted a new line of reasoning in the discussion and moved the problem-solving process forward, leading to teammates sketching out new diagrams and equations. As they and the other teams worked, Sheila moved around the room listening in on students' conversations. When it appeared that most had reached a consensus, Sheila pulled the class together and asked three teams to present their work to the class. She'd selected the teams based on her observations during the small-group discussions, purposefully choosing teams that had different solutions or different approaches to solutions in order to generate a class discussion that would build conceptual understanding and clear up any misunderstandings.

As each team presented their work, Sheila encouraged responses from the other students: "Mikayla, how does this solution compare with your team's work?" "Pham, do you agree with the approach that's being used here?" "Luisa, these two teams used the same approach but arrived at different answers. Can they both be correct?" Her thoughtful probing pushed students to defend their thinking and use evidence to support their reasoning for one another. "The best moments in these discussions are when you see the lightbulb go on and a student 'gets it,'" Sheila reflected. "And those moments invariably come in response to what another student has said or a question that one of their peers has asked. It is far more powerful when they teach each other and learn together instead of having it all come from me."

[Cookie-Cutter Problem Solution: In case you are wondering about the answer to the math problem in Sheila's class, there are a number of "correct" diameters, including ½-inch, 1-inch, 2-inch, 3-inch, and 4-inch cookie cutters. As students discovered through their discussion, all cookie cutters with diameters that are factors of twelve will generate equal amounts of waste. See Figure 4.3.]

Unpacking the Cookie-Cutter Problem: Characteristics of Authentic Listening and Speaking

The listening and speaking that students engaged in during their quest to solve the cookie-cutter problem in Sheila's class approximate the oral communication that is required in the world beyond high school. To make sense of their work, students needed to truly listen to and understand ideas presented by their peers, articulate their own thinking using language appropriate to the discipline, and engage in constructive dialogue to build consensus. Doing so increased their involvement in the lesson, deepened their conceptual understanding, and strengthened their listening and speaking skills. How does a teacher like Sheila get students to this point? A close examination of the lesson reveals that Sheila had thoughtfully designed the learning with the principles listed in Figure 4.4 in mind.

Figure 4.3. Cookie–cutter problem solution.

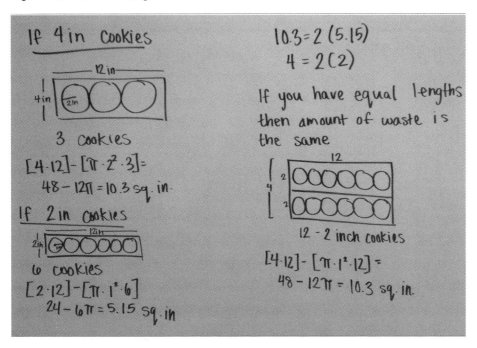

Authentic Discipline-Focused Inquiry

The listening and speaking that we ask students to do in the classroom need to have a genuine impetus. In professional life, higher education, and civic participation, we talk because we are working to solve real problems; the same opportunities need to be afforded to students in high school. Certainly there are times when we want students to engage in short "turn-to-your-neighbor-and-talk" and "think-pair-share" conversations for the sake of checking answers, brainstorming responses, or clarifying understanding in the midst of a larger lesson. But these short and sweet conversations need to be supplemented with opportunities for more in-depth, inquiry-oriented dialogue that prepares students for the oral communication demanded after high school while also building deeper content learning.

The problems that students respond to in Sheila's classroom are intentionally designed to support in-depth conversations. Termed *open-ended problems* by math education researchers, the cookie-cutter problem and others like it are mathematical problems that can be solved in more than one way or may have more than one solution (Schuster & Anderson, 2005). These open-ended problems are designed to develop analytical, creative, and critical thinking skills as students work to build

Figure 4.4. Instructional strategies that support authentic listening and speaking in the disciplines.

- **Authentic Discipline-Focused Inquiry**
  - Structure learning around open-ended or essential questions.
  - Engage students in collaborative problem solving that provides a real reason for them to talk to one another.
  - Reflect discipline-appropriate communication norms.
- **Teacher as Facilitator**
  - Encourage student-to-student talk in which students respond directly to one another.
  - Avoid the teacher impulse to provide "the answer." Step into student-to-student conversations only to push students to go deeper by refocusing, asking probing questions, providing additional details, or redirecting when needed.
  - Set students up for oral communication success by intentionally teaching both the content knowledge and the speaking and listening skills needed before the discussion or presentation begins.
- **Structured Instruction and Support**
  - Provide models and explicit instruction around listening strategies, presentation skills, and the use of discipline-specific academic vocabulary.
  - Teach students to recognize how to adapt their use of language, structure, and tone for varying formats and contexts.
  - Use self-assessment and peer evaluation to help students analyze their oral communication skills and recognize their progress.
- **Practice, Practice, Practice**
  - Provide regular opportunities for students to engage in both listening and speaking in the classroom.
  - Vary oral communication structures to respond to a variety of topics, purposes, and audiences.

on their prior knowledge, postulate new approaches to problem solving, and respond to dead ends they may encounter when an idea doesn't work out (Forsten, 1992; Jarrett, 2000). In other disciplines, similar opportunities are afforded through what Wiggins and McTighe term *essential questions*: questions designed "to stimulate thought, to provoke inquiry, and to spark more questions" (2005, p. 106).

As with open-ended problems, essential questions have more than one answer, can be approached in more than one way, and are designed to uncover the complexity of the topic under study.

To effectively respond to open-ended problems, essential questions, or other forms of authentic inquiry, effective communication and collaboration are more than just a helpful aside; they are an integral part of the learning. "The problem-solving teams are critical for both my high achievers and my struggling math students," Sheila reports. "When they have a problem like this they have to work together. It is more than just having the high achievers explain it to the strugglers, which is what happens with the average textbook problem and just serves to perpetuate the stereotypes these kids bring with them to class. Because these problems are complex, almost no one 'gets it' right away, and they have to puzzle it through together. Often it is the questions asked by some of the struggling students that prompt the group to see the problem in a new way and move forward toward a solution."

> **Teaching Tip**
>
> When you are designing inquiry-oriented questions that promote authentic speaking and listening, a helpful litmus test is the "dinner table" conversation test: if this is a question that would prompt debate around the family dinner table, then it is likely a good candidate for promoting discussion in the high school classroom.

Listening to their peers and collaborating to respond to inquiry-oriented problems also help students develop the ways of thinking that are specific to the discipline. In math this includes mathematical reasoning skills that encourage systematic analysis and a mathematical disposition that allows for flexibility and a willingness to persevere through challenges that may initially appear to students as insurmountable (Jarrett, 2000; Strong, 2009). "When we first started doing the problem-solving teams, I sometimes felt like just giving up," one of Sheila's students acknowledges. "But I learned that when you start to talk it through, you can usually figure out a solution."

In other content areas, the structure of the oral communication in the classroom will and should vary in response to the ways of thinking in the discipline. In the social sciences, for example, there are often competing claims and evidence, and much of what these disciplines demand is for its practitioners to be able to sort through and evaluate information and ideas to determine which claims hold greater sway in a particular context. In school, then, teachers who create structured opportunities for students to discuss issues with peers can help them to develop the analytical knowledge and skills to recognize and assess claims, weigh evidence, and articulate their understanding. History educator Diana Hess observes, "Discussion can teach students how to articulate their understanding of a question, explain their arguments, listen to how others think through the same question, and challenge others' responses. In short, discussion can help students think through the complicated dimensions of a complicated world" (2004, p. 153).

Designing successful inquiry-oriented discussion that stimulates authentic disciplinary thinking is not always easy. Sheila admits that she spends hours developing questions, which sometimes still don't hit the mark. "There's nothing worse than thinking you've got this great question only to have students look at it and come up with an answer straightaway," she laughs. But when the questions or problems are effective, they can prompt authentic opportunities for meaningful listening and speaking while also deepening students' content understanding.

Teacher as Facilitator

"When a colleague comes in and tells me that my classroom runs so easily, I don't know whether to laugh or cry," Sheila comments. Classrooms where students are actively engaged in learning that effectively incorporates listening and speaking often do appear "easy" to the outside observer since the students are doing most of the talking and the teacher is less visible at the front of the room. But, as Sheila will be the first to acknowledge, facilitating the effective use of talk in the classroom requires thoughtful planning, a deep understanding of the content, and a considered awareness of students' strengths and needs for both their content knowledge and their oral communication skills.

In her investigation of discussions in the high school classroom, Katherine Simon found that the teacher plays a pivotal role in the creation of meaningful discussions. She reports that discussions often fail to result in meaningful learning because teachers shut them down prematurely, whether out of fear of losing control or an unwillingness to cede the floor to the students (2001). Commenting on Simon's findings, educator Diana Hess notes that they "illustrate a significant barrier to quality discussion: it is impossible to create good discussion if teachers talk too much. Not only does teacher monopolization of the talk prevent students from having an opportunity to participate, it also communicates to students that their ideas are not valuable" (2004, p. 152). Of course, this is not to suggest that teachers should remain silent during discussions in the classroom. Indeed, a good facilitator is required to ask deliberate questions, interject new information, or share a different perspective to advance the discussion,

Teaching Tip

A simple clipboard can be a helpful tool in encouraging student-to-student discourse. Getting students to respond to one another rather than look to the teacher for answers can be a challenge. Taking notes on a clipboard during class discussion sessions serves two functions: (1) it sends students the message that they will be held accountable for their participation, and (2) it provides a physical barrier to your participation, a place for you to look so that students begin to look at one another rather than you when they respond.

redirect the focus when needed, and deepen students' thinking (Nystrand, Wu, Gamoran, Zeiser, & Long, 2003).

In addition to the work that goes on *during* a discussion, a significant amount of teacher facilitation is required *before* a discussion or student presentation to ensure success. "Most of the students think I'm wandering around with a clipboard just to monitor their participation," Sheila comments about her role during the team problem-solving portion of the lesson. "And yes, I am doing that. But I'm also assessing where students are getting stuck and what misconceptions seem to have taken root. I'm making notes on which teams have tried out some interesting solutions that should be presented to the full group. And I'm writing down notes for myself about the questions that I should ask during the discussion to push their thinking." This on-the-spot assessment of student learning, combined with a clear vision of her goals for students' learning and an ability to walk the tightrope of direct involvement during the discussion between participating too much and not contributing enough, allows Sheila to ensure that discussions are meaningful speaking and listening opportunities that further students' content learning.

Structured Instruction and Support

Although students have been listening and speaking since infancy, the kind of talk that is required in the high school classroom is quite different from the conversations students engage in outside of class. Academic discourse is often more formal in its tone and structure, with discipline-specific demands in language use and terminology. And, as literacy expert Maria Nichols notes, "The heightened level of engagement necessary for purposeful talk may be something new to [students]" (2006, p. 29). To support success in students' effective speaking and listening in the classroom, teachers must intentionally teach the norms and skills of what Lauren Resnick refers to as "accountable talk" (1999). In classrooms where students engage in oral communication that is purposeful and that supports content learning and discipline-appropriate ways of thinking, not only is talk modeled by the teacher in her or his interactions with students, but it is also "deliberately taught, nurtured, and expected" (Allington & Johnston, 2001, p. 205).

Unfortunately, whether because we assume that students already know how to communicate, we don't have time, or we don't feel comfortable teaching communication skills, we tend not to provide the same level of attention to this important aspect of disciplinary literacy. Lucy Calkins observes that in the elementary and middle schools where she works, "talk is sometimes valued and sometimes avoided, but—and this is surprising—talk is rarely taught. It is rare to hear teachers discuss their efforts to talk well" (2001, p. 226). The absence of explicit instruction in oral communication is particularly problematic for English language learners

Teaching Tip

Initially students may roll their eyes at the idea that they have to learn how to talk. Bringing in a student from a previous year or a professional from a related field to share with students the differences between informal conversation and academic, discipline-based discourse will help promote buy-in and establish a clear purpose for the work.

and struggling students, many of whom may not have significant exposure to academic language and more formal registers of communication outside of school. For these students, intentional language instruction has been found to be especially critical in helping them to understand the expected norms of communication and to develop the language needed to succeed in the classroom and in the workplace (August & Shanahan, 2006; Goulden, Nation, & Read, 1990).

The focus of oral communication instruction can include everything from active listening strategies to presentation skills to specific academic vocabulary. In her classroom, Sheila explains, at the beginning of the year she spends quite a bit of time setting norms and teaching students how to talk and listen in their teams. "They are used to talking socially," she comments, "but they need strategies for being able to listen and respond to one another when they are talking about math." Together the class establishes norms for their work, including "Give everyone a chance to share their ideas. Don't interrupt while someone else is talking. Ask questions." Sheila also teaches her students language they can use when responding to one another, such as "So what I hear you saying is . . . ," "I wonder if you've considered . . . ," and "Let's try it another way. . . ."

As the year progresses, Sheila continues to make time to explicitly focus on students' oral communication development. Students regularly engage in self- and peer evaluations, reflecting on their contributions and setting goals for how they can strengthen their listening and speaking skills in the future. (See Chapter 5 for examples of these kinds of evaluations.) Sheila teaches and reminds students to use the academic vocabulary needed to present their thinking with appropriate mathematical precision. She also video-tapes the class and occasionally plays excerpts of team discussions or group presentations during a targeted mini-lesson, asking students to assess what is working, what can be done better, and how they can apply their learning. "The video is a real eye-opener for students," Sheila comments. "For many of them there is a big disconnect between their perception of how well they communicate orally and the reality. Getting them to recognize what is working and what isn't is an important step in improving their oral language abilities."

Practice, Practice, Practice

Research studies consistently highlight not only the importance of preparing students with the oral communication skills necessary for life beyond high school, but also the importance of meaningful listening and speaking in supporting learning in the classroom. A 1997 study by Nystrand and his colleagues found a positive correlation between the amount of student discourse in the classroom and performance on knowledge-based exams. A 2005 study by Wolf, Crosson, and Resnick found that effective classroom talk was linked to a high level of students' thinking and active use of knowledge. A 2006 report by the Center on English Learning and Achievement (CELA) concludes that "learning is most effective when classrooms emphasize knowledge derived from active participation in meaningful conversations within important fields of study" (qtd. in Nichols, 2008, p. 13).

To realize these positive results in the classroom today and prepare students for success in higher education, the workplace, and civic and community life in the future, students need regular opportunities to practice listening and speaking in academic contexts. Practice needs to include a range of structures, audiences, and topics. Students need to regularly give formal presentations, engage in small-group collaborations, and participate in whole-class discussions. In Sheila's classroom, students work in teams to solve open-ended problems at least once and usually twice each week. The frequency of these discussions is necessary for students to maximize the benefits. "At first they struggle to figure out how to talk to each other about math," Sheila observes. "But as they practice, they become more and more proficient and the focus really gets to be on the math rather than the dynamics of the conversation. They are able to dig deeper into the concept and truly learn from one another."

As part of the classroom approach to solving open-ended problems, Sheila's strategy of requiring two to three groups to present their process to the class provides students with additional speaking and listening opportunities. The presentations, while focused on the topic just discussed in their teams, provide a different structure and somewhat larger audience for the students. Since they haven't yet been in dialogue with the whole class around this problem, presenters have to be more deliberate in how they choose to represent their group's thinking. They cannot assume that others approached the problem the same way and therefore they need to use graphic representations and terminology more precisely. Sheila is thoughtful in how she cycles students through these mini-

Teaching Tip

It can be difficult to recognize student progress in oral communication when you are in the midst of teaching, especially since speaking and listening can be harder to document than other aspects of disciplinary literacy. You might try inviting a colleague or administrator to visit every month or so. This impartial observer's presence can help you recognize your students' evolving strengths, provide another perspective on overcoming any challenges you may encounter, and demonstrate to students that other adults also prioritize oral communication and recognize their progress.

presentations, ensuring that all groups have regular opportunities to share with the whole class and requiring rotating leadership responsibilities within the groups so that every student has a chance to be heard.

An additional speaking and listening opportunity for Sheila's students occurs several times each year when they are required to give more formal presentations to external audiences as part of the school's interdisciplinary project-based learning program. They work in groups to respond to challenges involving math and science and then present their findings to parents, teachers, and community members. Sheila reports, "The first time they have to do a PBL [project-based learning] presentation, they are terrified. But we practice and we practice, and they realize that the speaking and listening skills we've been working on every week in our math classroom can transfer to these presentations as well. It's pretty awesome when they actually present. They are so proud of themselves. All of that practice pays off."

Classroom Portraits of Authentic Listening and Speaking

How might teachers in other disciplines use these same four learning principles—authentic inquiry; teacher as facilitator; structured instruction and support; and practice, practice, practice—to create opportunities for authentic speaking and listening? In the following classroom portraits, you will meet teachers in various content areas and grade levels as they create speaking and listening opportunities for their students. As you read, consider how these characteristics manifest in these classrooms. And then consider how you might apply the questions in the following list to designing meaningful speaking and learning instruction in your own classroom.

- **Authentic Inquiry.** Do students have a real reason to engage in speaking and listening? How will talk strengthen their conceptual understanding and build discipline-appropriate ways of thinking?

- **Teacher as Facilitator.** Is there an appropriate balance between teacher guidance and student ownership of academic talk in the classroom? Does the teacher purposefully design the speaking and listening opportunities for success?

- **Structured Instruction and Support.** Is there targeted instruction to teach speaking and listening skills? Is attention given to the language, structure, and tone demanded for varying formats and contexts?

- **Practice, Practice, Practice.** Do students have opportunities to regularly engage in listening and speaking in the classroom? Do these opportunities include listening and speaking in both formal and informal contexts?

Physics Demonstrations

For the past five years, Brett Haas's high school physics class has partnered with the physical science class at the middle school across the street. Every month or so, classes from the two schools engage in an exchange program of sorts, with the high schoolers presenting interactive demonstration lessons for the middle schoolers. The presentations are themed around the broad conceptual strands in the physics curriculum: motion and forces, conservation of energy and momentum, heat and thermodynamics, waves, and electric and magnetic phenomena.

Midway through each of their physics units, Brett's students work in teams to plan a series of focused demonstrations that can help the middle school students build conceptual understanding. For a recent unit on force, student teams developed demonstrations to describe forces such as gravity and friction, explain interactions between forces, and explore the impact of mass and velocity. Although all of the demonstrations must be responsive to the physics curriculum, the specifics of the focus and design of the demos tend to vary around students' interests and the questions the material has raised for them. For example, one team decided to take on the challenge of examining centripetal force using a water-in-the-bucket demonstration. "When I was younger, my older brother used to torture me by threatening to dump a bucket of water over my head," one student in the group recalled. "Then he would do this thing where he would swing the bucket in a circle over his own head but no water would come out. I remember being amazed that he could do that. Our group decided to use that demonstration because we knew it would be a good way to connect with the middle school students to teach about centripetal force" (see Figure 4.5).

Oral communication skills are critical to the success of these demonstrations. First, Brett's students need to successfully communicate with one another as they identify their focus, design the demo, and prepare for their presentation. Second, the students need to successfully communicate to their middle school audience, interacting with them in a way that effectively communicates core concepts while also keeping them engaged and motivated to learn.

"To engage the middle school students in the content, my students really have to know the concepts and be adept at communicating their ideas in a manner that responds to the unique demands of their audience," Brett explains. "They have to be prepared to introduce and then explain their demonstration, be ready to respond to student questions that sometimes come in from left field, and know how to think on their feet to explain things differently if the younger students are confused or are just not getting it." At first, presenting to middle school students can be a challenge. After all, twelve- and thirteen-year-olds do not always listen

Figure 4.5. Slide from student presentation on centripetal force.

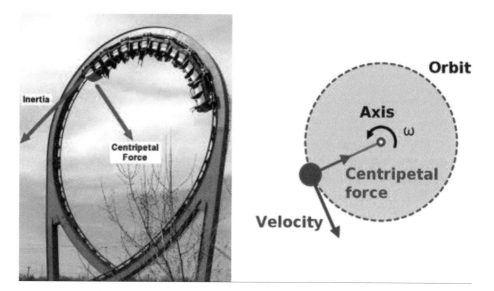

politely, and they will call you out if you aren't clear or if you are making things up. But as the year progresses, the demonstrations become stronger and stronger, with both groups of students coming to look forward to the interactions.

Brett supports his students in preparing for their presentations by modeling sample presentations (both good and bad) and then deconstructing what worked and what didn't. He shares videos of presentations from previous years that were particularly strong and provides students opportunities to practice their presentations with their peers before they present to the middle schoolers. After each set of presentations, he elicits feedback from the middle school students and their teacher: What did they like? What was not so great? What did they learn? What questions did they have? Responses to these questions, combined with self-assessments from the high school students, are then used to inform the design and presentation of the next set of demonstrations.

Brett has found that the demonstration lessons, in addition to improving his students' presentation skills, have had a dramatic impact on his students' content knowledge. "You know that old adage about how if you really want to learn something you should teach it . . . ? Well, that is what these students are doing. They are teaching students who are a little bit younger than they are, and in the process, they are learning the material backwards, forwards, and inside out. They are becoming the experts." On standardized test scores, Brett's students routinely outperform their peers, and in surveys, a higher percentage of them indicate that they are interested in continuing to study physics or a related field. One alum from Brett's class explained, "I never would have thought I'd be interested in studying physics or engineering before this class. Before, physical science always seemed really abstract. But when we were teaching the demo lessons, I found that I was able to make the material relatable and to see how it could be practical in the real world. I really liked seeing the impact it had on the middle school kids, and now I think I want to study physics in college."

Election Videos

Election season provides rich opportunities for Chris Hilliard's grade 12 government students to apply their learning in an immediate and meaningful way. In 2012 the seniors collaborated with the local chapter of the League of Women Voters (LWV) to create campaign videos to educate and engage the youth vote. Teams of Chris's students created a series of three- to five-minute YouTube videos that informed prospective voters, ages eighteen to twenty-four, about races for city council and judgeships, provided background on candidates vying for state and federal offices, and educated young people about California's numerous (and often confusing) ballot propositions. "The youth vote is always a challenge," LWV representative Nona Adams explained. "In a presidential election year, they are more likely to turn out but often don't know anything about the down-ballot candidates and issues. Our hope is that by partnering with students who are new voters or soon-to-be voters, they will be able to speak to this demographic in a manner that those of us who are a little older don't seem to be able to do very well."

To create the videos, students worked in teams of three on a focus race or proposition. They intentionally chose races that hadn't garnered much media attention but were important in influencing policy that would impact the lives of young people. Although all members of the team needed to work together to conduct their research, for the video itself each team member took primary responsibility for one element: one provided background information, one presented the "pro" candidate's position, and one represented the "con" candidate's stance. When initially assigned, the project seemed fairly straightforward, but as they worked through the research, students realized just how complex our system of government actually is. "I thought I knew what a judge does, but the more I researched the office, the more I realized how different their job is than what I actually expected," one student commented. Along the way, students worked with LWV members to ensure accuracy of information and avoid privileging one side or the other in their presentation. "It seemed like every way we turned we got conflicting information," another student observed. "Having Mr. Hilliard and the LWV representatives there to bounce ideas off of helped us clarify our understanding before we committed anything to video."

As students began to put together their videos, they realized that although they had had plenty of previous experience giving presentations, and although they themselves were in or near the target demographic of the videos, speaking to an invisible audience through a one-way electronic medium was vastly different from any presentation or conversation they had had before. Students needed to develop a new repertoire of speaking and listening skills to be successful in this project. With video there is no audience feedback; unlike a face-to-face presentation in which students could adjust and adapt in the moment in response to visual clues from their audience, with video they had to anticipate audience responses carefully to ensure that they captured and held the audience's attention. Additionally, the relative permanence of video and the reality that it could be watched again and again or sent to a potentially huge audience meant that accuracy was essential, so most of the students decided to script their parts. But in presenting the video, they had to make sure that they didn't *appear* scripted, which would turn off viewers, particularly young viewers, and damage their credibility.

To help students develop these new skills, Chris invited a local news anchor into the classroom to teach some of her tips. He also had students watch and analyze news and entertainment shows that were popular with the target demographic, such as *The Daily Show* and *The Colbert Report*, to better understand how to balance delivering information with engaging the audience. And he provided lots of opportunities for students to practice, encouraging them to use their smartphones to practice their "on air" delivery in order to develop a voice that was both compelling and trustworthy for their target audience.

At the same time that students were learning how to speak to a youth audience on camera, they were also learning to hold professional conversations with more mature individuals face to face. Chris noted that "the LWV proved to be a very involved partner on this project, and students learned some important lessons about how to listen, present their ideas strategically, and, on a few occasions, disagree respectfully." Chris worked with student teams before they met with LWV voters to think through conversations and help them develop the diplomatic listening and speaking skills they would need for success in this project and will undoubtedly need to apply again in academic, professional, and community settings in the future.

The videos, posted online a couple of weeks before the election, were promoted via the LWV website, local news outlets, several of the candidates' ad campaigns, and social networking. In total they received more than 1,200 hits before the election as well as hundreds of "likes" and positive comments from viewers, including, "Really helpful. Thanks!"; "I feel much better prepared to go into the ballot box"; "Great job. Very informative"; "I was going to vote for president but now I'm also going to vote for my local and state representatives"; and Chris's favorite, "Wish my high school gov class would have done something like this!" Viewership of one of the videos really took off several weeks after the election when a newly elected official who had been featured as a candidate in the video was caught up in a scandal that made the national press. Suddenly, the number of hits multiplied exponentially, and the video's creators saw their faces on TV, prompting Chris to design a new set of lessons on media and politics.

Reflecting on the project after the media buzz died down, Chris and his students unanimously declared the project to be a success. My observations in the classroom support their declaration. The project strengthened students' knowledge about the levels and branches of government and the process of democracy. It built listening and speaking skills responsive to a twenty-first-century media environment. And it developed disciplinary-specific literacy understanding, shaping students into much more savvy political media consumers and producers. "Knowing that we were going to be on the Internet made me care much more about making sure we were providing accurate information," commented one student. "I made an effort to look at multiple sources before claiming anything on the video." Another student noted, "I have a much better understanding of elections now and really understand what people are talking about when they describe the challenge of running for office." Another student reflected on the eye-opening nature of the project: "We had to be really careful when we were presenting on the videos to share the opinions of the candidates or the proposition supporters without advocating for them. I learned a lot about the fine line between informative and persuasive speech, and I realized that a lot of what people in journalism claim to be informative is really persuasion masquerading as objective reporting."

Literature-Based Socratic Seminars

At least twice each week, students in Sonia Garcia's tenth-grade English class move the chairs into a large circle to engage in Socratic seminar–style discussions. The space is a bit crowded and, at the beginning of the year especially, the conversation can be somewhat stilted, but Sonia is dedicated to ensuring that her students know how to participate in meaningful literature-based discussions.

Sonia's motivation for prioritizing this kind of instruction comes from her own experience. The first of her family to complete high school and graduate from college, Sonia started out in the publishing business. Right out of college she went to work as an assistant editor with a large publishing house, assigned to first-reads on unsolicited manuscripts. In many ways, it was her dream job. As a child growing up in a poor community, Sonia had often found escape in the books she checked out from the library. Now she was being paid to read books, although admittedly, many of them weren't particularly good. But Sonia never really felt as though she "fit" into the publishing community. When the other members of the editorial team would meet formally to discuss manuscript reviews or chat informally about the progress of particular authors, Sonia often had trouble finding her voice. "The meetings when we were discussing purchasing decisions would get particularly heated," Sonia explained. "Everyone else seemed so confident, jumping in with their comments and opinions about the manuscripts and the authors, but I would often sit there tongue-tied. I had good ideas but I never managed to voice them effectively."

It wasn't until she went to family dinner at the home of one of her colleagues that Sonia realized the problem wasn't her knowledge or intelligence, but rather a difference in experience:

> Her family had these loud, wide-ranging discussions during dinner. They talked about politics, books, and movies. Everyone participated, even the children. It was great preparation for the kinds of discussions we had at the office . . . and it was totally different from my experience growing up. My dad worked three jobs and my mom often left food in the oven for us when she went to work in the evening. My sisters and I would eat in front of the TV. My parents loved us and worked incredibly hard for us, but their version of preparing us for success was to feed us and send us to school. We didn't have experience talking to each other the way they did at [my colleague's] dinner table.

Now a high school English teacher, Sonia is determined to provide her students, many of whom come from backgrounds similar to her own, with the experience and social capital needed for effective oral communication in their future academic and professional careers. Through Socratic seminars, she aims to create a metaphorical dinner table conversation in her classroom. "I want them to learn how to effectively engage in academic conversations now so that they are able to use their voices to build their careers and create change in their communities in the future."

Sonia intentionally designs classroom instruction to set her students up for success. Knowing that this kind of academic discourse is unfamiliar for many of her students, Sonia explicitly teaches them language structures and conversational norms. They analyze video and transcripts of successful literature discussions from high school classrooms and college campuses, looking for the use of probing questions, clarifying questions, meaningful connections, and text-based evidence. They learn the difference between evidence, argument, and explanation in both oral and written conversation. They learn sentence stems designed to insert new ideas into the conversation, to respectfully disagree, to bring other voices into the discussion, to refer back to the text, and to question the assumptions behind others' arguments (see Figure 4.6).

Figure 4.6. Socratic seminar sentence starters.

Socratic Seminar Sentence Starters

★ "I wonder/think/believe..."

★ "The author asserts that..."

★ "On page #___ it states..."

★ "Have you considered..."

★ "I hear what you are saying but..."

★ "What evidence do you have to support...?"

★ "Another way to think about this is..."

★ "I agree with ___ that..."

★ "___ what do you think about...?"

★ "Can we all agree that...?"

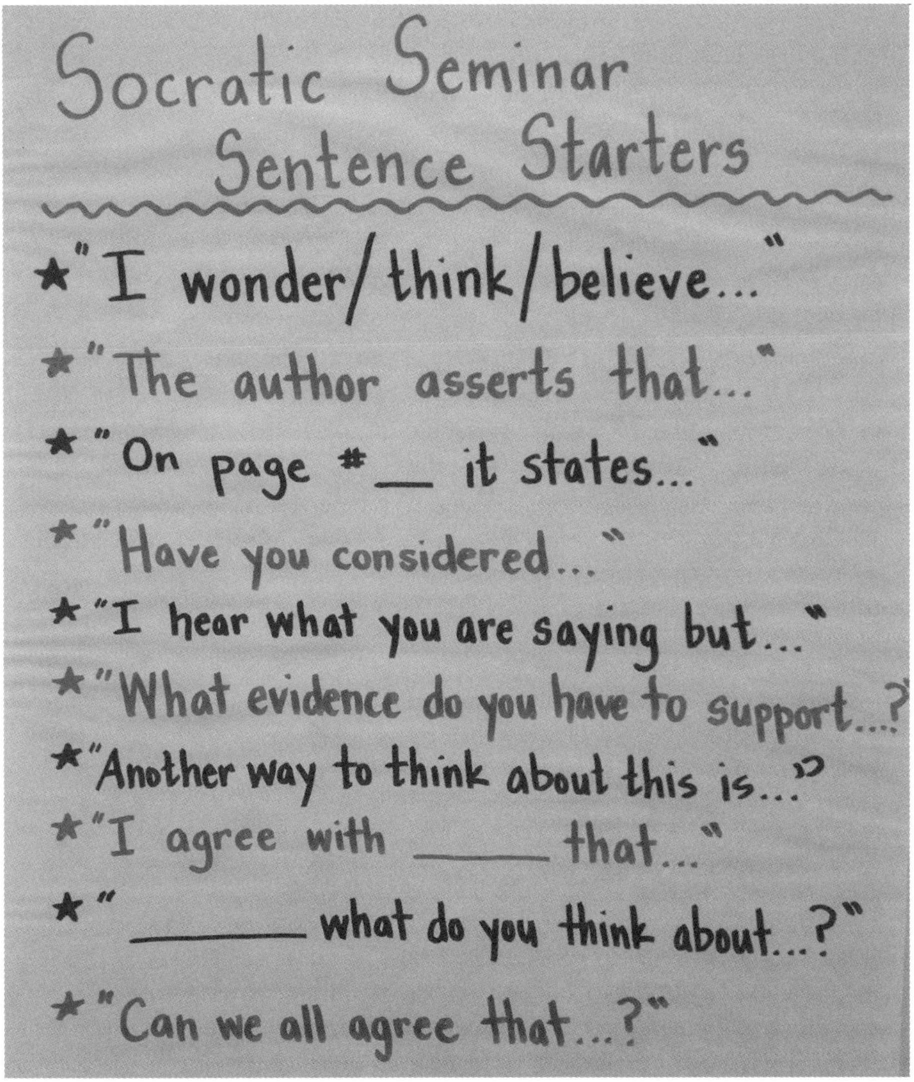

At the beginning of the year, Sonia builds Socratic seminar discussions around shorter, more accessible texts that are layered around a theme or idea. "Students have been so trained to expect that there is only one answer to a question that if I only use one text or ask one guiding question, then I will only get one or two students to participate and then they will look at me expectantly, thinking they are done," Sonia explains. Early discussions might involve a collection of four to five Langston Hughes poems, a short newsmagazine article on a topical concern paired with a handful of quotes from classic literature, or even a picture book complemented by magazine photos. During the discussion, Sonia brings in the texts one at a time, framing the introduction of each new text in a manner that extends the conversation.

This past fall Sonia opened a discussion focused on an article about the role of technology in learning by stating, "This article seems to suggest that technology could interfere with our ability to think deeply about ideas. How do you respond?" She then listened and took notes as students shared their ideas, stepping in on occasion to remind them to connect directly with the text: "I really like where this is going. Kiara, Alejandra, and Tyler all shared similar ideas. I'm wondering if there is evidence from the text that you specifically agree or disagree with." Or "Juan Diego, your comment seems to connect with the quote at the top of the third column. What do you think?" When the conversation slowed and began to repeat itself, Sonia brought in a quote from *Walden*, offering an alternative perspective on the topic that encouraged students to think more critically about the nature of learning. "Thoreau wrote a long time ago," she noted. "Do you think this is still relevant?" Later she brought in quotes from Albert Einstein and Aldous Huxley and then reconnected with the original article. In total the conversation lasted nearly thirty minutes, a solid sustained conversation that was much longer and more meaningful than most these students had encountered up to this point in their educations.

Before initiating a Socratic seminar, Sonia primes the pump by providing all of the readings and materials to students ahead of time. "My students process at different paces," Sonia comments. "I have English language learners and some special needs students who need more time to read and prepare. I have other students who need to read a text multiple times to really understand, or who need to read it slowly and really chew on it." Sonia distributes and provides time in class to read and individually respond to each of the texts a day or two in advance of the seminar discussion. She also gives students graphic organizers that help them think through the comments they might make in advance of the discussion. "For some of my students, it can be scary to insert themselves into the conversation," Sonia notes. "Preparing possible comments in advance helps them feel more confident to participate in the discussion" (see Figure 4.7).

Figure 4.7. Socratic seminar preparation guide for students.

<table>
<tr><td colspan="2" align="center">**Socratic Seminar Prep Guide**</td></tr>
<tr><td colspan="2">Name: _____   Text: _____   Date: _____</td></tr>
<tr><td>Main Idea(s)</td><td>Text Evidence</td></tr>
<tr><td>My Comments</td><td>My Questions</td></tr>
</table>

As the year progresses, conversations flow more readily and Sonia transitions to longer texts and novels. She continues to focus explicitly on teaching oral communication skills, encouraging students to self-assess their individual and the class's progress, videotaping and collaboratively critiquing their work, and training students to use assessment guides to monitor conversations in process (see Figure 4.8). She also works individually with students who struggle, helping them practice their oral communication skills in smaller group settings and inviting them to engage in less formal conversations during her weekly lunchtime movie discussion club.

By the end of the school year, Sonia's class buzzes with academic conversation from the moment the bell rings. "When other people come in and see the class discussing Shakespeare or Fitzgerald in-depth, they are always amazed," Sonia explains, beaming with pride. "The perception is that these kids can't have those conversations, but the reality is that they are smart and capable. We just have to give them the tools." Sonia reports that the Socratic seminars also strengthen her students' reading and writing abilities, and her class's standardized test scores

Figure 4.8. Guides for assessing student participation in Socratic seminars.

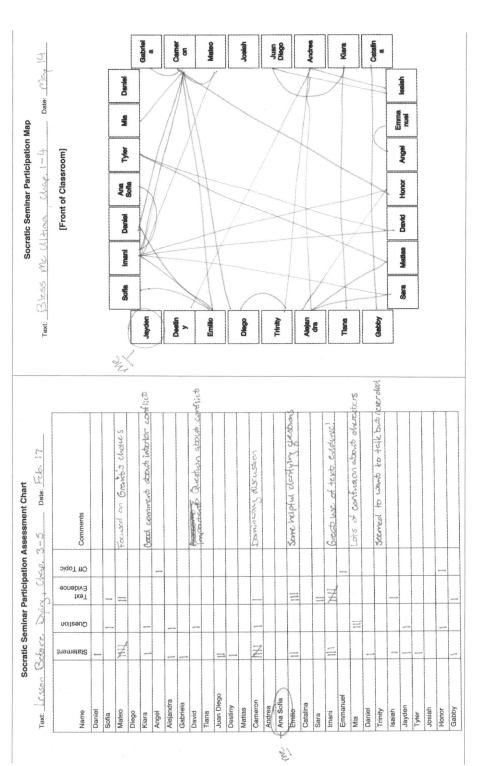

certainly support that conclusion. Most important to her, however, are the reports that students bring when they come back to visit after they graduate from high school. "When a student tells me that they weren't afraid to speak in a college discussion or that they've become a leader in their class or at work, it just means the world to me. What we did in the classroom helped them learn to use their voice."

Connection to the Common Core State Standards

The instructional practices described in this chapter closely align with goals established by the Common Core State Standards for Speaking and Listening. Both emphasize the need for students to be able to engage in purposeful oral communication that encourages effective collaboration and presentations. Both prioritize students' ability to speak and listen in a range of formal and informal contexts and effectively use appropriate academic language. The expectations set by the CCSS also highlight the need for students to evaluate information, analyze a speaker's point of view, and be able to effectively integrate and respond to digital media and digital displays of data. To achieve all of these objectives, instruction that is deliberately designed to strengthen students listening and speaking skills, like the instruction described in this chapter, is essential.

College and Career Readiness Anchor Standards for Speaking and Listening, Grades 6–12

Comprehension and Collaboration

1. Prepare for and participate effectively in a range of conversations and collaborations with diverse partners, building on each others' ideas and expressing their own clearly and persuasively.
2. Integrate and evaluate information presented in diverse media and formats, including visually, quantitatively, and orally.
3. Evaluate a speaker's point of view, reasoning, and use of evidence and rhetoric.

Presentation of Knowledge and Ideas

4. Present information, findings, and supporting evidence such that listeners can follow the line of reasoning and the organization, development, and style that are appropriate to task, purpose, and audience.
5. Make strategic use of digital media and visual displays of data to express information and enhance understanding of presentations.
6. Adapt speech to a variety of contexts and communicative tasks, demonstrating a command of formal English when indicated or appropriate.

(Common Core State Standards Initiative, 2012, p. 48)

Meaningful Assessment and Critique

Tamika Young and the other members of the supply chain distribution management team at a midsize manufac-turing company get together to review PowerPoint slides for an upcoming presentation. Each member of the team shares the two to three slides they've been responsible for creating and gets feedback from the group mem-bers on content, style, and structure. Although they've done the drafting of the slides individually, they will be held accountable as a group, so it is important that all of the work is high quality and that the slides fit together seamlessly.

Linda Wilson, an office manager with a small chain of retail stores, participates as both a reviewer and a re-viewee in the company's semiannual employee review process. During the process, employees are required to complete a self-evaluation and then to work with their supervisor to set goals for professional growth. Although Linda knows how hard it can be to be honest in self-evaluation, her experience has demonstrated that those employees who can be self-critical and reflective are likely to be the ones who will advance.

Candidate for city council Manuel Espinoza has knocked on hundreds of doors and shaken thousands of hands over the past three months. Along the way, amidst slammed doors and disinterested glares, he's had plenty of time to reflect on his presentation and tighten his pitch—learning how to quickly size up an audience, grab their attention, and get to the point. He'll need all of those skills and more at the first candidate debate at a local elementary school auditorium later this week. In preparation, he's holding late-night practice sessions with a team of friends and informal advisors. Some of their critiques are hard to hear, but he knows that his success is largely dependent on listening to and learning from their feedback.

Freelance technical writer William Singh relies heavily on the interactive features of Google Docs to get feedback and advice from colleagues, prospective readers, and clients. By sharing draft documents, William is able to ensure that he is accurately representing information and in a manner that is appropriate for its target audience. He has found that capturing the feedback from prospective readers is also valuable when presenting a finished product to the client since it allows him to demonstrate that he is responsive and that the documents will effectively serve their purpose.

Assessment, Critique, Professionalism, and Personal Accountability

As the economy has shifted toward the information age and now, according to some, the imagination age, the ability to assess your own work, provide and respond to constructive criticism, and reflect on and take ownership of your progress has become a critical skill. Members of a collaborative team, such as Tamika Young and her colleagues, need to be able to work together, provide feedback to one another, and find ways to strengthen one another's work. Employees and supervisors such as Linda Wilson need to be able to reflect on their performance and consider how they might improve. Entrepreneurs and self-employed innovators such as William Singh and aspiring politicians and advocates such as Manuel Espinoza must seek out and respond to critique to ensure that their communication effectively represents their ideas and is responsive to its intended audience. Reflection, self-assessment, and responsiveness to critique are essential components of professionalism in the workplace. They demonstrate maturity and a sense of personal accountability that is highly sought after among employers and is cited in surveys as a key determinant of success in both higher education and the workplace (Peter D. Hart Research Associates, Inc./Public Opinion Strategies, 2005; Casner-Lotto & Benner, 2006; National Association of Colleges and Employers, 2012).

Unfortunately, though highly prized, professionalism and personal accountability are often judged to be lacking among recent high school graduates. In a 2006 survey of 400 employers, 80.3 percent of respondents described these characteristics as "very important," but 70.3 percent found that recent high school graduates were deficient in these areas (Casner-Lotto & Benner, 2006). These descriptions of high school graduates were consistent across type of industry, size of company, and region of the country. One human resource manager bemoaned the lack of new workers' ability to self-assess, commenting that recently hired graduates often felt entitled to more than they were realistically prepared for and that many were unwilling to put in the time and effort to move up. "Kids want to get that top job right away, the nice air-conditioned office with the computer—never mind that the way managers achieved those jobs was by starting at the bottom and working their way up. . . . Just because they made good grades on a test doesn't necessarily make them good employees."

For those of us who are around high school or college-age students on a daily basis, these critiques can seem harsh, even untrue. We've seen what great people our students are and have hope in the next generation. But the surveys cited earlier make it clear that our perceptions are not universally shared. How can we help students to more clearly demonstrate their willingness to self-assess, take feedback, and work hard to achieve? Closing this gap will not only help our students be more successful in college and careers, but it will also help them be better leaders and contributors to our communities.

"School" Assessment and Critique

Limited time, crowded classrooms, standardized test pressures, and a sense of professional responsibility mean that much of the assessment and critique that take place in high schools is done by teachers rather than by students. We assess students on tests, essays, and projects. We provide critique in the form of grades, rubric scores, and, sometimes, detailed commentary. In our best moments, we are able to use those assessments to plan instruction and guide differentiation of student support. These are all good practices and critical elements of effective teaching and learning in the classroom. But if we teachers are the *only* ones doing the assessing, we are missing an opportunity to teach students to gauge their own success and take responsibility for their own learning. In *An Ethic of Excellence*, Ron Berger writes, "Most discussions of assessment start in the wrong place. The most important assessment that goes on in a school isn't done *to* students but goes on *inside* students. . . . How do we get inside students' heads and turn up the knob that regulates quality and effort? How do we affect assessment so that students have higher standards for their behavior and their work?" (p. 103). Similarly, in their review of literacy practices and research, the Alliance for Excellent Education advocates for more opportunities for students to engage in practices that promote self-assessment and critique, noting, "Students need to be self-regulating not only to become more successful academically, but also to be able to employ their skills flexibly long after they leave school" (Biancarosa & Snow, 2006, p. 16).

Beyond the workplace mandate, we know that when we don't engage students in the process of self-assessment and peer critique we lose important opportunities to support students in their disciplinary and literacy learning. Some of the most enduring learning goes on during the review and revision process. When students recognize their own strengths and weaknesses through self-assessment and peer critique, they become much more focused on ensuring that they have a full understanding of the content so that they are able to communicate it effectively.

Some of my favorite comments from students come when they have "aha" moments about their disciplinary learning in the midst of revising a paper or presentation and then make the comment, "I wish someone had told me this earlier." I'm never sure whether to laugh or cry when I hear this since the students nearly always have been "told" this earlier—but until that moment of production and presentation, they often weren't fully processing the information. Critique that comes from peers or through their own reflection is often more meaningful than information that comes from their teacher (Graham & Perin, 2007), and when students realize through a critique process that they don't yet have a full grasp of the information, they are more likely to dig in and master the content, especially if the expectation is that they will be presenting this content to an external audience.

Engaging students in an assessment and critique process that more closely approximates expectations beyond high school has multiple potential benefits:

1. It helps students to develop habits of accountability, self-regulation, and reflection.

2. It serves to strengthen students' reading, writing, listening, and speaking skills.

3. It promotes mastery of content learning.

4. It helps to distribute both the burden of assessment and the ownership of the quality of the work among both students and teachers.

Ultimately, real-world assessments have to do with how the message of the work is received by the audience for which it is intended. The more teachers make use of project-based learning that is shared with real audiences and experts in the field (the kind of work described in this book), the more opportunities students will have to experience these real-world assessments. Self-assessment and peer critique are two strategies that help prepare students for those experiences.

Of course, to be effective, self-assessment and peer critique practices need to be thoughtfully structured. We've likely all participated in peer feedback sessions that lacked buy-in or purpose and ended up feeling like a waste of time. When well designed, however, such opportunities promote powerful learning in general and disciplinary understanding specifically, as the following example, taken from an English classroom, demonstrates.

Meaningful Assessment and Critique in the High School: An Example

During the memoir unit in Stephanie Anderson's ninth-grade English class, each Thursday is dedicated to peer critique. Organized into groups of four, students share samples of their memoir-in-progress following a strict protocol. Taking turns, each student-author begins the critique process by introducing his or her writing, describing the intended audience and purpose, explaining progress thus far, and asking peers to pay particular attention to one or two areas of concern. Peers then read through the memoir silently, taking notes that highlight areas they particularly like, offering suggestions, or asking questions when confused. Once the reading is complete, discussion begins. Peers are expected to first provide "warm feedback," i.e., comments about aspects of the text that they find particularly interesting, thought provoking, meaningful, or descriptive. "Cool feedback" follows, with students making observations and asking questions about areas of the text that are confusing, don't fit the author's purpose, or may be underdeveloped. Conversation then turns to the areas of concern the author highlighted before wrapping up with specific suggestions the author can use to improve his or her writing (see Figure 5.1 for Stephanie's peer critique protocol).

Throughout the feedback discussion, the student-author is expected to step back from the group, physically and metaphorically. He or she remains in close

---

Figure 5.1. Peer critique protocol.

---

1. Organize the group.
   a. Select a discussion leader and a timekeeper.
   b. Determine the order of author-presenters.

2. Introduce your writing—(2 min.).
   a. Share your work—Type in the email addresses of your group members and allow them to "view" your Google Doc.
   b. Provide background—Describe your intended audience and purpose, progress you have made since your last peer critique, and any challenges you've encountered.
   c. Set a purpose—What area(s) would you like the group to focus on?

3. Read the text—(10 min.).
   a. Group members read the text silently and take notes.
   b. Presenter slightly removes him- or herself from the group, remaining within hearing distance.

4. Group discussion—(10 min.).
   a. Warm feedback—Group members share what they like about the text.
   b. Cool feedback—Group members share questions or concerns they have about the text.
   c. Suggestions—Group members make suggestions that can help the author improve the text.

5. Reflection—(3 min.).
   a. Presenter rejoins the group.
   b. Presenter shares reflections on what he or she heard from the group discussion and discusses plans for next steps. Group members listen only.

6. Repeat steps 2–5 with a new presenter.

enough proximity to hear everything that is said, but that bit of physical distance helps to prevent the author from injecting him- or herself into the discussion prematurely. "It seems like such a small thing, but I've found it to be a critically important component of the success of these feedback groups," Stephanie observes. "If the author can hold their tongue, then the group can have a much more thoughtful discussion and often comes up with some fantastic recommendations that are really useful in the revisions. But if the author keeps stepping in to defend their work, then the other students are much more reluctant to offer meaningful critique. It can really stifle the conversation."

A snippet of discussion from one Thursday critique group demonstrates how thoughtful student feedback can be:

> **Brittany:** I like this section here where she's describing why this dinner with her dad was so important to her. It shows why it matters and helps make it into a memoir instead of just a nice story.
>
> **Kris:** Yeah, but I wonder if some of those ideas could have been introduced earlier. It feels like kind of an add-on at the end.
>
> **Alex:** I agree with both of you. I like this part at the end but I am also kind of surprised by it. There isn't enough foreshadowing. She needs to put some clues into the story earlier so that we can see where it's leading up to.
>
> **Kris:** I wonder if she added a bit more here when she says she doesn't see her dad often. Right now that is kind of a throwaway, but if she added a sentence or a phrase to show how not seeing him makes her feel, that could help set up why it matters so much to have her dad take her to dinner later on.

At the conclusion of the peer discussion, the student-author is invited to reengage with the group. Authors can offer a response to anything they've heard during the discussion but are encouraged to avoid a point-by-point rebuttal and focus instead on the suggestions they heard that they want to incorporate into their writing. "We want them to consider how to use the feedback they've received to improve their memoirs," Stephanie explains. "It takes modeling, practice, and sometimes individual conferences with me to get students to the point where they are able to really hear the feedback, assess its relevance, and apply it to their writing. This is a learned skill but one that is worth developing."

Getting students to successfully engage in the peer feedback protocol is similarly a learned process. Successful teachers introduce this early in the school year and practice it regularly, not just during the memoir unit. Some students are uncomfortable at first but most come to appreciate the feedback they receive. "At the end of this unit, we are going to publish our memoirs and present them at Authors Night," one student explains, referring to the end-of-unit culminating event. "Our principal will be there, our parents are invited, and Ms. Anderson said that some authors and publishers might come too. The memoirs have to be really, really, really good, so the feedback we get now is really important." Another student agreed, commenting, "This is our memoir and it is up to us to make sure that we communicate our experience to the audience, but sometimes it is hard to know if what you write will show what you want it to show. It can be hard to hear your friends talk about your writing, but it is important because it helps you learn to be a better writer."

Unpacking the Memoir Unit: Characteristics of Meaningful Assessment and Critique

Students in Stephanie's class approached the process of assessment and critique with maturity and professionalism. Hearing critique from their peers not only strengthened this specific piece of writing, but it also helped them to develop writing skills that transfer to other genres and contexts. And the practice of regularly engaging in critique helped to develop their critical reading skills, listening and speaking skills, and ability to self-regulate and be thoughtful in their reflection and assessment. Unpacking the teaching and learning that occurred in Stephanie's class reveals the characteristics of meaningful assessment and critique experiences that can be applied across content areas, grade levels, and school settings (see Figure 5.2).

Grounded in Strong Discipline-Specific Models

To facilitate effective assessment, peer critique, and self-reflection, it is essential that teachers and students share clear and transparent expectations about the kind of work that is required. Having a vision of the end goal, understanding what content knowledge is to be demonstrated, and recognizing the discipline-specific literacy expectations help to facilitate meaningful critique of work in progress. McManus (2008) explains that for feedback and revision to be effective, students must be able to answer three questions: (1) Where am I going? (2) Where am I now? (3) How can I close the gap? Students need clear expectations to be able to respond to the first question, and these expectations are a prerequisite for answering questions two and three.

In Stephanie's classroom, an essential component of establishing clear expectations involves the use of models. For the memoir unit, students examined,

---

Figure 5.2. Instructional strategies that support meaningful assessment and critique.

- **Grounded in Strong Discipline-Specific Models**
  - Establish clear and transparent expectations for student work.
  - Communicate content knowledge and discipline-specific literacy demands that students should demonstrate.
  - Use models of similar work in the discipline to help students understand expectations and consider how the models might apply to their own work.

- **Opportunities for Revision and Improvement**
  - Provide feedback at all stages of the creation process—from brainstorming to drafting to polishing—before a final presentation or paper submission.
  - Provide time in class for students to revise their work in response to feedback.

- **Direct Student Involvement in the Review Process**
  - Involve students in peer critiques and self-assessments. The teacher should not be the only one assessing student work.
  - Establish protocols, processes, and norms to support students in giving feedback.
  - Hold students accountable for their participation in peer critique and self-assessment.

- **Practice, Practice, Practice**
  - Work toward a culture of student-driven excellence.
  - Provide multiple opportunities for students to engage in assessment and critique during individual projects and activities, as well as in evaluating their progress over the course of a semester or year.
  - Value the process of peer critique and self-assessment by recognizing students' effort and participation.

---

analyzed, and critiqued multiple texts, including published memoirs by world-renowned authors such as Maya Angelou and Henry David Thoreau and sample memoirs by other students found online and in collections written by Stephanie's previous students. Working together in discussions facilitated by their teacher, the students drew information and ideas from these models to develop standards and expectations that would guide the writing of their own texts. They discussed what made memoirs unique, how this genre differs from other narrative or expository writing, as well as how it is distinct from writing in other disciplines. They identified literary devices that other authors used effectively in their memoirs and considered how to apply these techniques in their own writing. And they critiqued other authors' work, noting when material became confusing, what information was superfluous, and how the work could be improved (see Figure 5.3).

Figure 5.3. Student-created list of the characteristics of memoirs.

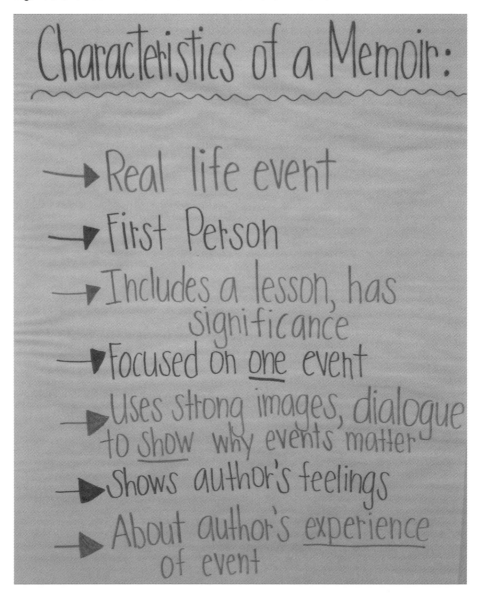

Teacher and consultant Ron Berger, an expert in supporting the facilitation of peer critique, comments that models are essential to establishing expectations and encouraging the creation of high-quality work: "There is almost no area where models don't increase the quality of what we do. We assume that if we explain a project clearly enough in words, then kids will know where we want them to go. But it almost never works that way. In the absence of a model and a picture and a vision of what we want the final product or performance to be, even the clearest rubric is not particularly useful" (2008, n.p.).

> ## Teaching Tip
>
> Sometimes it can be helpful to provide students with a less effective example alongside the effective discipline-specific models. Analyzing a sample that provides misinformation or fails to cite evidence, for example, can help students recognize how the model texts avoid these failings and effectively integrate accurate and relevant information.

One of the concerns often voiced about the use of models is that students may be limited by the model or that they will merely copy the ideas and be unwilling to develop their own independent approach. Stephanie shared similar fears when she first began using models but has found the opposite to be true:

> When I provide students with a series of strong exemplars, it is actually liberating. It helps [students] imagine what is possible. Some do borrow ideas from one or two of the models, but I figure that is okay, as long as they are making conscious decisions, giving attribution where it is needed, and contributing significant ideas of their own. After all, what writer or artist or engineer doesn't borrow ideas from those who have come before? That's part of the creative process.

Opportunities for Revision and Improvement

For assessment, critique, and reflection to be meaningful, students must have opportunities to apply the feedback directly to their work before the final deadline. This seems obvious, but our time-crunched, coverage-driven classrooms often prevent us from fully embracing this approach in practice. Teacher and literacy expert Kelly Gallagher comments, "It has been my experience that if you want to see a student's work improve, you have to provide the student with meaningful feedback *before* the paper is finished. What benefit is there to students when we suggest changes after their papers are completed?" (2006, p. 148). Gallagher draws on Doug Reeves's comparison between teaching and training boxers. Reeves terms the practice of focusing primarily on final evaluation as "sucker punch grading" because it "resembles the blow delivered to the unsuspecting boxer who does not see the devastating punch until it is too late to offer a defense" (2006, p. 115). Gallagher extends the analogy, commenting, "We need to be in our students' corners *during* their writing bouts. It does adolescent writers little good for the teacher to show up after the final bell has rung" (p. 148).

Revision has, of course, long been part of the standard writing process; it comes right after "outlining" and "drafting" on those writing process posters that adorn many classroom walls. But actual writing rarely follows such a neat progression, and between time pressures and overcrowded classes, revision in schools too often gets reduced to a reminder to check grammar and spelling before submitting a final product. Teachers then end up lugging those final products around (both physically and metaphorically), carrying them back and forth between school and home. When we finally buckle down to grade student work (usually late at night or over the weekend), we may spend hours writing carefully worded comments, only to have students glance at the grade and then throw the paper in the trash when it is returned to them. Their reaction, while frustrating to us, is a reasonable response to being "sucker punched." It is hard to read criticism, and if students don't see the feedback as something they can immediately apply to yield a better result, they are unlikely to take the time to seriously consider and learn from the commentary, no matter how carefully phrased.

In Stephanie's classroom, students had multiple opportunities to receive meaningful feedback while in the process of creating. The peer critique process occurs periodically from early on in the memoir writing process, helping students to refine their work all along the way. "Our first critique session in this unit focuses on the students' seed ideas," Stephanie explains. "If we wait until they already have a draft, it is too late. They need to get feedback early so that they are open to making changes and are continually checking themselves to see if their writing fits their purpose and audience."

Stephanie further supports her students' revision efforts by building time into the class for rewriting. Peer critique sessions are typically held on Thursdays, which provides opportunities on Fridays for students to engage in revising, reworking, and polishing their writing. A classroom observation at the end of the week finds students working individually or in small groups to revise their writing. They use notes from the critique session as well as notes from previously taught mini-lessons to guide their work. Stephanie makes her way around the classroom answering questions, offering encouragement, and holding individual writing conferences where needed to provide definition or focus to the previous day's critique. Having this time in class helps to ensure that students apply the feedback from the previous day to their

Teaching Tip

Obviously we don't have time in the school day for every piece of student work to go through an intensive revision process. These processes should be prioritized for work that is designed to reflect the authentic demands of the discipline and will be shared with a larger audience. Focus on fewer pieces that emphasize deep knowledge and high quality.

revisions. As one student, a self-professed "hater" of writing, commented, "What else am I going to do? We have to be in class and we aren't doing anything else, so I might as well make some changes." Plus, the student grudgingly admitted, "the revisions do make it better. I actually like some of the things I've written this year."

Direct Student Involvement in the Review Process

Feedback from a teacher can be powerful, but critique that comes from students has the potential to be transformative. Elisabeth Soep, a producer with youth radio, has found that when students are actively engaged in the critique process, they are afforded a level of authority typically reserved for teachers or advisors and that this empowers them to become actively invested in the quality of the work. She observes, "The more students evaluated their own work as it developed, using criteria presented at the beginning of the task, the more motivated and task focused was their discourse, resulting in higher quality products and more sophisticated written reflections" (2006, p. 749).

Additionally, direct student involvement in the critique and reflection process is essential if the revision efforts are to deepen content understanding and strengthen disciplinary learning. The old adage that if you really want to learn something you need to teach it reflects an essential truth: we learn content with much greater purpose if we are responsible for ensuring that it is effectively communicated. When a teacher provides feedback, students may make the changes suggested, but they often do so as quickly and with as little thought as possible in order to fulfill what the teacher told them to do and move on. Far more meaningful are self-reflections that encourage students to recognize (and fill in) gaps in their own understanding, and peer critique sessions require students to explain their thinking to one another and to consider how different understandings of a concept may work together or how to resolve conflicts if their representations contradict each other. These discussions help to uncover misunderstandings and deepen content learning.

In Stephanie's classroom, direct student participation is integral to the assessment and critique process. Stephanie laughs when she comments that the students do her work for her: "There's no way that I could do this all on my own. I don't have enough hours in the day to sit down and have the kind of critique session with each of these students that they are able to have

> **Teaching Tip**
>
> A safe classroom environment is essential if students are to engage in meaningful critique and self-assessment. It is never easy for students to be vulnerable enough to share and honestly critique their work in progress. You can help support their willingness to do so by establishing and maintaining classroom norms around respect, developing relationships with students that recognize their individual strengths, and modeling a willingness to be vulnerable enough to share your own work (even when it isn't perfect).

when they work in teams." But utilizing peer critique teams is about far more than distribution of labor. By involving the students, they come to understand the literacy learning expectations, they take ownership of the outcomes, and they learn self-regulation strategies. "I like this class because it's like we're all responsible for our work," one student observed. "In other classes, the teacher tells you what to do and gives you grades, but here we work together to make our work better. It helps you understand more and makes you care about doing a good job."

Of course, not all peer critique and self-assessment opportunities are created equal. Absent clear guidance, critique sessions can feel rudderless, with students giving feedback to one another that is lacking in direction and specificity. For critique to be effective, protocols need to be adopted, processes need to be taught, and norms must be established. In Stephanie's classroom, critique and reflection are purposefully cultivated. From the beginning of the year, Stephanie prioritizes the critique and revision process. She teaches the critique protocol explicitly and then works with students to establish norms for participation (see Figure 5.4). She provides opportunities for students to reflect on their engagement with their critique teams, redirects when needed, and holds students accountable for active involvement in and constructive application of the feedback received from their peers. These reflections are further supplemented at the end of each unit, when students are asked to describe the revisions they have made to their work and self-assess the impact of peer critique on their learning. Note: because Stephanie uses computers and online writing in this classroom, forms are submitted online using Google Forms (see Figure 5.5).

Stephanie notes that getting students to dig into the critique and move beyond "It's good" is one of her greatest challenges. "They are so afraid of hurting each others' feelings. And many of them initially just don't have the language to give feedback that is specific and helpful without being mean. It is a learned art to give good feedback. But what they discover when they learn to do it well is that critique helps everyone. It helps the student whose work is being reviewed and it helps the reviewers too." This was clearly evidenced during a critique session when Brendan, a student who had been struggling with his own writing, stopped himself in the middle of discussing the memoir of another student, Jocelyn, to consider how he could improve his own: [Regarding Jocelyn's work] "The description of the dinner really needs to show more details. Right now it just tells us what they are eating, but if the point is that they are coming together across cultures, then it needs to show how the different foods taste so that we can understand the differences and the similarities. . . . [Brendan slaps his palm on his forehead and turns to another student in the critique group] Oh! This is what you were trying to tell me before about my description of catching that wave. I can't just tell you I caught it, I have to explain how it felt and show why it mattered. I get it now!"

Figure 5.4. Student-generated peer critique norms.

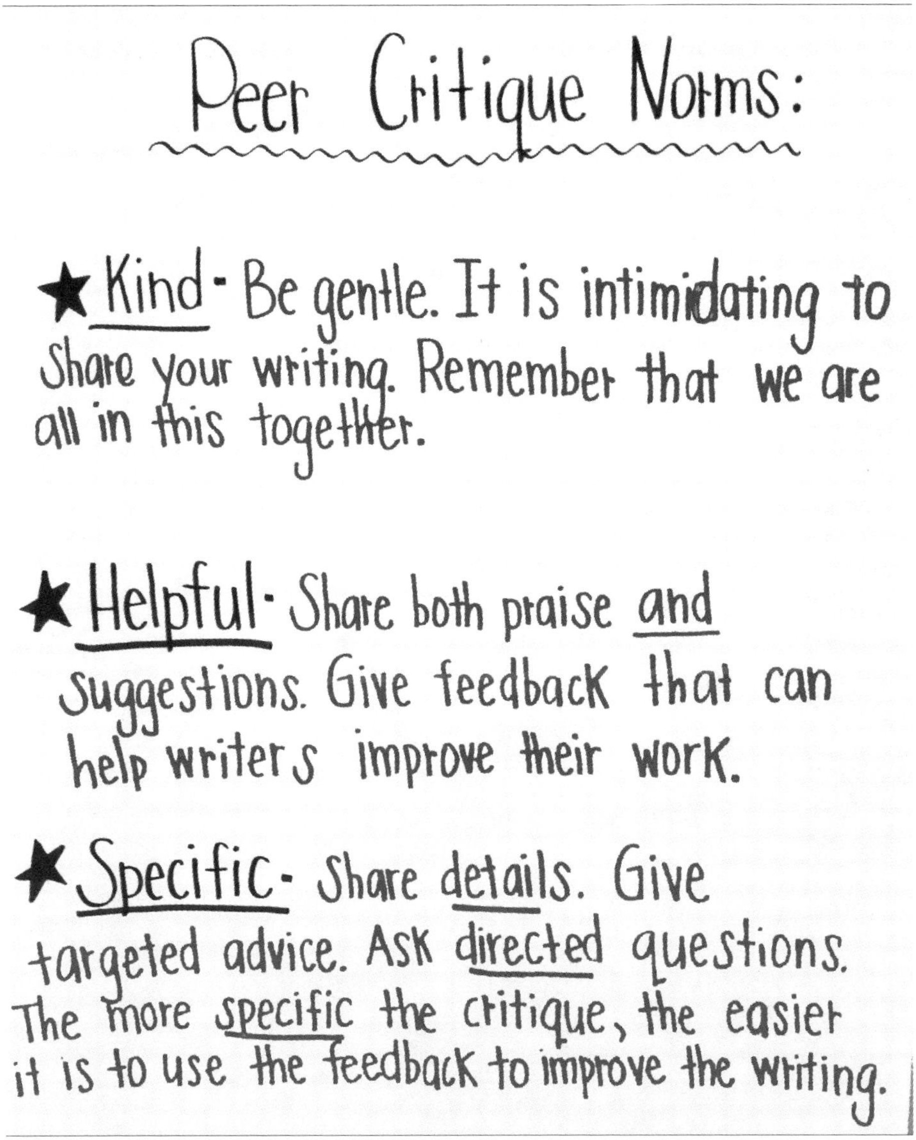

Peer Critique Norms:

★ <u>Kind</u> - Be gentle. It is intimidating to share your writing. Remember that we are all in this together.

★ <u>Helpful</u> - Share both praise <u>and</u> suggestions. Give feedback that can help writers improve their work.

★ <u>Specific</u> - Share <u>details</u>. Give targeted advice. Ask <u>directed</u> questions. The more <u>specific</u> the critique, the easier it is to use the feedback to improve the writing.

Figure 5.5. Peer critique reflection sheet.

Peer Critique Reflection

New Learning
What did you learn from today's critique session?

Contributions
What did you contribute to supporting your peers?

Applications
How will you apply your learning from today's critique session to strengthen your own writing?

Submit

Never submit passwords through Google Forms.

Practice, Practice, Practice

To be truly effective, assessment and critique cannot be one-time activities; they must become part of the culture of learning. Teaching students to reflect, critique, and revise requires significant initial investment. By the time students reach high school, they are often disengaged from the assessment process and accustomed to relying on others to determine their level of success for them. Breaking those expectations and creating a new culture that empowers students to participate in the process of establishing expectations, critiquing quality, and determining achievement requires multiple opportunities to practice assessing their own work and the work of others. In some schools, such as the High Tech High schools, Central Park East Secondary School, or the Coalition of Essential Schools, student-driven assessment and critique are part of the fabric of the teaching and learning and are often credited as a critical component of school reform and student success (Benitez, Davidson, & Flaxman, 2009; Meier, 2002).

Stephanie works to grow a culture of student-driven excellence from day one. She begins by asking students to reflect on work they've created that makes them proud. She requires them to set individualized learning goals and holds quarterly conferences with each student to assess their progress toward those goals. Routine peer critique sessions and self-evaluation are hallmarks of all papers, presentations, and projects in the class. And public exhibitions of student work provide opportunities for students to calibrate their expectations for themselves and their own work against the expectations of others. She notes that this work can be time consuming and frustrating but believes that in the end it is worth it: "Every year there are moments where I question if this is really going to work. Maybe this year or this class I should take another approach because they just don't seem to be getting it. But every year they surprise me. And when the student who always wants you to tell her the answers starts critiquing her own work, or the kid who comes to you at the beginning of the year filled with self-doubt swells with pride because he can see that he's done a good job, that's when you know that it's working." Ron Berger notes that when students like those in Stephanie's class take responsibility for their own learning and work to achieve excellence, education can be transformational: "Once a student sees that he or she is capable of excellence, that student is never the same. There is a new self-image, a new notion of possibility. There is an appetite for excellence" (2003, p. 65).

Teaching Tip

Students need to see that their revision efforts make a difference. Maintaining portfolios that document work at different stages can help students recognize their progress. Encouraging them to reflect individually and collectively on the impact of revision can encourage students to take ownership over their use of critique and revision as core learning strategies.

Classroom Portraits of Meaningful Assessment and Critique

How can you, as a content area teacher, learn from the approaches Stephanie uses in her classes to create new ways to approach meaningful assessment and critique? The examples described in the following sections provide windows into assessment and critique practices in a range of classrooms, grade levels, and content areas. Some take place in schools where student-driven assessment is part of standard operating practice. In other situations, teachers work on their own to create a culture of student ownership around assessment and revision practices. As you read, consider how each of the characteristics described in Figure 5.2 and in Stephanie's classroom applies to varying contexts and practices. And then use the questions in the following list to consider how you might apply the characteristics to assessment and critique in your own classroom:

- **Grounded in Strong Discipline-Specific Models.** Are expectations for student work clear and transparent? Are the models grounded in discipline-specific literacy norms?

- **Opportunities for Revision and Improvement.** Are opportunities in place for students to get feedback on their work while it is in process? Can time be allocated in class to ensure that feedback is used to guide revision?

- **Direct Student Involvement in the Review Process.** Do students play a role in assessing their own work and critiquing the work of their peers? What protocols and norms need to be established to ensure that self-assessment and peer critique are effective?

- **Practice, Practice, Practice.** Do students have multiple opportunities to engage in the process of assessment, critique, and revision throughout the year?

Sustainable Energy Project Presentations

The students in Jamie Wilson's grade 9 Earth science class fidget in their high heels and ties. They weren't required to wear such fancy clothing, but each has come dressed in his or her finest. Today Jamie's students will be sharing their final presentations for the spring trimester sustainable energy project with panels of community leaders and industry experts. Each team of students will share their research into global energy challenges and propose a sustainable energy solution. They will be assessed on the accuracy of their content, the originality and feasibility of their proposal, and the design and delivery of their presentation. A lot rests on these presentations. Students' grades will be informed by the reviewers' comments. Perhaps more important, these students are invested in the proposals they have developed and take pride in knowing they have the potential to contribute to a larger conversation around sustainable energy solutions. Their fidgeting reveals their concern that their ideas and their presentations be well received.

Many of the panelists are familiar to the students by now. Some of the community leaders have attended the students' presentations in previous trimesters, and a number of the industry experts have made appearances in the classroom during this unit to share their knowledge of the field, model presentations they have made at academic conferences and for potential funders and government agencies, and give feedback to students on earlier iterations of their proposals. "I initially volunteered to come in just the one time to share some of what our company is doing with solar energy," an executive with a local solar energy company explained, "but I was so impressed with the questions the students asked and their engagement with the project that I've come back three other times. Their enthusiasm is infectious." A project scientist from another company agreed, stating, "When I first came to the panels three or four years ago, I honestly didn't expect much. After all, these kids are just fourteen and fifteen years old, so I wasn't anticipating that they would have any earth-shattering ideas. But I've been consistently impressed by the thought and originality of their proposals. We're actually hiring one of the students who presented last year as an intern this summer to work on our algae biofuel project."

When the presentations begin, the room grows quiet as the first team of presenters begins with poised, confident voices that belie the nerves present a few minutes earlier. "Good morning. Welcome to our presentation on geothermal energy . . ." the first group begins. The calm they are able to project comes from deep investigation of their topic and multiple feedback sessions. The teams have been working on this project off and on for the past three months. As the class studied units on thermal energy, wind and ocean currents, and radiation and convection together, student teams took notes on which aspects of the unit applied to their area of focus. As their investigations became more specialized, they sought out print and online materials to further their knowledge and invited guest speakers into the classroom in person and via Skype to share up-to-date developments in the sustainable energy field. These same guest speakers became resources when students began to develop their own proposals; Jamie encouraged his student teams to email experts in their field with their early ideas to see if they were on the right track and get suggestions for how to strengthen their proposals. As students began to formalize their proposals and prepare for presentations, they revisited videos of the guest speakers' presentations, this time analyzing them for structure and style to understand the norms and expected dynamics of science-focused presentations. Students practiced their presentations in front of their peers, receiving critical feedback that helped them reframe their information and tweak the details to ensure that they were effectively communicating their ideas to their intended audience. Some even went so far as to video their presentations, play them back, and analyze their delivery for clarity, eye contact, tone, and use of visual supports in an effort to be professional in their approach for the final presentations.

During the presentations, guest panelists score students using a feedback rubric that assesses both content and presentation design and delivery (see Figure 5.6 for a sample presentation rubric). The rubric is very familiar to students—it's the same one they used during peer critiques and self-assessments in their practice sessions. This time, of course, the feedback "counts" toward the final grade but, recognizing that the panelists' comments provide valuable learning information, Jamie requires students to read and respond to the comments and then factors the quality of the students' reflections into their final project grades. Even though most won't be revising and re-presenting this presentation, there are still valuable take-aways that can inform future presentations, as evidenced in the following student's reflection:

> The feedback from the presentation surprised me. I had gone into it thinking that our information was really clear. We had lots of facts and since this was a science presentation I thought that was most important. But the questions from the panel and the feedback on the forms showed that the audience had a hard time understanding the overall idea of our proposal. Looking back, we included too many facts. I don't think we did a good enough job of explaining the goal of our proposal. If we were to do it again, we would need to have a stronger focus on the big idea and then explain how our information connects to that big idea. I learned that even in a science presentation, the ideas have to be clear and that *how* you present the facts matters.

After the student presentations, Jamie thanks the panelists and then breathes a big sigh of relief. Planning for and hosting the presentations involves many moving parts and can be stressful for both teacher and students, but Jamie finds that the benefits far outweigh the challenges:

> Presenting for an audience makes the work real in a way that in-class presentations never seem to quite manage. I'm always amazed at how much the students learn through the critique and revision process in the days leading up to their presentations. They focus much more closely on the details of the science, learning to effectively use terms that they struggled over just a few weeks earlier. Suddenly they are able to articulate the details of a chemical process, distinguish and explain processes such as convection and conduction, and make connections between their proposals and the laws of thermodynamics. They also become more confident in their presentation skills. They learn to make eye contact and speak in a clear and measured voice. By the time of the presentations, some of them amaze even me with the strength of their knowledge and the quality of their presentations.

Guest panelists are similarly impressed, with comments including the following: "Some of the presentations rival work that I hear when I go to scientific conferences"; "These kids are scientifically literate in a way that puts the general public to

Figure 5.6. Rubric for the sustainable energy project presentations.

Sustainable Energy Project
Presentation Rubric

Rubric Scores
    4 =   Exceeds expectations
    3 =   Meets expectations
    2 =   Approaching expectations
    1 =   Below expectations

Category	1	2	3	4	Observations
Originality & feasibility of proposal • Creative & original idea • Attainable & affordable; is feasible to implement • Responsive to real concern			X		I really like that your proposal was targeted specifically to rural Kenya – small solutions are often the most powerful.
Use of evidence • Data is used to substantiate ideas • Information is accurate & clearly explained. • Citation of appropriate resources		X			Great information for your needs assessment. Additional data needed to support your cookstove design.
Presentation design • Proposal is clearly organized • Proposal is engaging and responsive to the audience • Media are used effectively to enhance audience understanding of the proposal.				X	Great use of visuals to support your proposal – The deforestation photos were especially powerful.
Presentation delivery • Presenters are personable and engaging (good eye contact, clear speaking voice, movements are purposeful) • All team members contribute • Questions are answered knowledgably and professionally				X	You all did a great job presenting your ideas – very professional! Great job answering some tough questions.

Overall Comments:

Your enthusiasm for your project is infectuous
You've come up with an original idea that
is affordable and has the potential to
respond to a significant environmental
challenge. Well done!

shame"; and "Even the weakest presentations are much more informative and in-novative than the work I did when I was in high school." Perhaps most important, the students themselves see the benefits of the work and recognize the growth that comes from the process of assessment and revision: "I'm really proud of our group and how far we came," one student observed. "The first time we did a practice pre-sentation we messed up on our facts and had to read everything off of index cards. By the time we did our final presentation, we knew our material so well that we could accurately answer questions from the panel." Another commented, "Having the time to get feedback, practice, and revise made a huge difference. We were able to really learn the information and design a presentation we are proud of. I feel like I mastered this material in a way that I'll remember for a long time to come."

Math Conferences

Two years ago Jennifer Long began experimenting with the flipped classroom con-cept. For their homework, students in her precalculus class watch videos on specific mathematical concepts that Jennifer has created or found and then they work collaboratively on problem solving in class. Although she found it time consuming when she first started this practice, Jennifer has also found that this inverted class structure allows her to differentiate instruction and teach for understanding much more effectively. Since inquiry-based, collaborative problem solving is a critical element of in-class instruction in the flipped classroom, Jennifer has been pur-poseful about teaching her students how to work together to engage in academic conversations. From the beginning of the year, she models the practice of articulat-ing mathematical thinking, demonstrates how to ask questions, teaches students to use diagrams and graphs to help explain their thinking, and coaches students while in the midst of their problem-solving discussions.

For the most part, students have responded well, learning quickly to work together in groups to solve problems. But around November or December of her first year using this approach, Jennifer realized that their collaborative problem-solving process had stalled and their growth stagnated: "They got into a kind of pattern where they would fall into different roles within the group," she observed. "Someone would take on the role of note-taker, someone else would take charge of the calculations, and someone else would focus on actually solving the problem. This usually worked to find a solution to the immediate problem, but it kind of defeated the point of working together. They weren't really learning from one another and deepening their conceptual understanding." Jennifer recognized that part of the challenge was in the problems she was asking students to solve and immediately sought out more complex problems that demanded greater collabo-ration. At the same time, she also decided to make students more aware of and hold them accountable for their engagement in the collaborative problem-solving process. She began holding quarterly assessment conferences with students that focused specifically on their growth as inquiry learners.

A recent problem-solving conference with one of her students, Pedro, started like this:

Jennifer: At our last conference, one of your big goals was to work on sharing your thinking with other members of your group. How is that going?

Pedro: I think I'm getting better. I've started to be a lot more careful to show my work when I'm working on a problem. I think one of the problems before was that I wouldn't write my work down when I first started to do the problem on my own, and then I'd get to the end and if people wanted an explanation of why I got an answer, I'd have to start again. Then I'd get frustrated and irritated. When I write my work down, it is easier for me to go back and explain it to others.

Jennifer: Wow! That's great, Pedro. I really like the thought you've put into responding to the goal we established at the last conference. I'm wondering if you see any additional benefits from writing down your work.

Pedro: Well, it takes longer so that's not really a benefit, but I have noticed that I'm getting more of my problems correct on our problem sets and higher scores on my tests.

Jennifer: I've noticed your scores have increased as well. I've always known that you could do the work, but lately it seems like the scores you get on tests reflect what you know and can do much more closely.

The conference continues for several more minutes with Jennifer and Pedro discussing additional areas of growth, problem-solving through some challenges, and setting goals for the next quarter. Before meeting with his teacher, Pedro, like all of his classmates, had completed a self-assessment form that requires him to reflect on his progress and consider goals for the future (see Figure 5.7). During his meeting with Jennifer, they will make adjustments based on their conversation, and then both teacher and student will sign the assessment form, signifying an understanding of agreed-upon goals and expectations. The forms are maintained in Pedro's portfolio to be shared during parent–teacher conferences and calculated into end-of-semester grades.

Figure 5.7. Self-assessment form for precalculus course.

Pre-Calculus Self-Assessment
Math Inquiry Learning

How frequently do you...

Category	Rating	Explanation for Rating
Mathematical Reasoning: • Use multiple strategies to solve problems. • Demonstrate flexibility in problem solving. • Employ inductive & deductive reasoning. • Generalize solutions to other situations.	3	*I'm learning to use more strategies in my work.*
Effort: • Come prepared to class. • Sustain focus throughout the problem solving process. • Follow through on individual & group assignments. • Take responsibility for seeking out additional resources as needed.	4	*I'm putting more effort into slowing down and showing my work.*
Collaboration: • Contribute ideas and strategies to the group. • Listen & learn from others' ideas and feedback. • Demonstrate respect for others' contributions & needs	3	*I still get frustrated sometimes but am learning to take feedback*

<u>Ratings</u>: 1 = Infrequently or not at all;   2 = Occasionally;   3 = Usually;   4 = Almost always;   5 = Consistently

Overall Self-Assessment of Learning-in-Progress:

Biggest accomplishment this quarter:

I've learned to slow down and be more methodical in my work. This has helped me get better at explaining my thinking and increased my accuracy.

Goal for next quarter:

Listen more carefully to the strategies my group members use. I tend to use one approach and I think I need to to learn to vary the way I think about a problem.

Student Signature: _____   Date: _____

Teacher Signature: _____   Date: _____

The conference process is time-consuming; Jennifer holds conferences for four to five days each quarter while students are reviewing for the end-of-term exams. But Jennifer firmly believes the time is worthwhile: "I've seen significant growth in students' math achievement since I started flipping the classroom, and I know that these conferences are a big part of that growth," she explains. "Students are much more self-aware than I would have expected. They report things to me during the conferences about their own learning or about my teaching that I never would have realized just from our day-to-day interactions. Having the opportunity to talk with them individually has helped me become a better teacher and helped me coach them to become better learners." Pedro agrees, stating, "I hadn't ever thought about how I solved problems; before I just did the problem and either I got it right or I didn't. When I had to assess my mathematical thinking for the conference with Ms. Long, it made me think a lot more about what I do to solve problems and how I could improve. I feel like it has made me better at math and now I like math a lot more."

Virtual Museum Display Revisions

"It looks like a lot of people liked our visuals," Jena reported.

"And we got good reviews for having interesting facts," Seth stated.

"But it doesn't seem like people got the point about how the weapons in World War I were very different from previous wars and how they changed the way that the war was fought," Kayley observed.

Jena, Seth, Kayley, and the other students in Keith Todd's tenth-grade world history class are reviewing the feedback they received from the previous day's peer review of their World War I virtual museum display. The class displays focus on various aspects of World War I, including the weapons of war, battles, the assassination of Archduke Franz Ferdinand, alliances, and the Treaty of Versailles. The students create the interactive displays as online websites in cooperation with the local chapter of Veterans of Foreign Wars (VFW). VFW members will be reviewing the displays, and the organization will post the ones they judge to be the best representations of history on their website as well as sharing them through a display screen at the local VFW hall. In addition, the chapter has offered a cash prize for the best display, an incentive that prompts even greater interest among the student teams in working to create engaging and informative websites on their World War I focus topic.

Keith had guided the class over the previous couple of weeks to support their research into the historical material as well as to help them determine how best to represent history through a museum display. They reviewed other virtual museum displays online, including sites from the Smithsonian, the History Channel, and National Geographic. They hosted a visit from the curator of the local historical society, who discussed some of the challenges when deciding how to represent history through a public display. And, after developing a common understanding of the broader context of World War I, each team of students drilled down into their focus topic, researching materials in the school library and online as they prepared to create their display.

The previous day's peer review was a dress rehearsal for the following week, when they would be sharing their displays with VFW representatives. During the peer review session, students used a series of guiding questions to review the web-sites created by their peers. Since the sites need to be able to speak for themselves, the creators of each site weren't allowed to provide explanation or rebuttal to the review. Instead, student reviewers worked in pairs to click their way through each site and then recorded their thoughts using an online form (see Figure 5.8). The feedback from all of the forms was then collected and became the subject of discussion for the design teams during this work session.

The goal for today's class session is to help students make meaning of their peers' feedback and determine how to use the critique to inform their revision process. Keith opens the class with an acknowledgment that it is often easier to give criticism than to take it, but he encourages students to give thoughtful consideration to the feedback from their peers since "it is much better to get feedback and be able to make changes before the work is presented to a larger audience rather than wait until after the site has its public debut!" He shares some of the feedback he received on the sample display that he developed and thinks aloud about the changes he needs to make: "I'm realizing that I have a lot of information on here that focuses on numbers and that for people who like numbers, like me, that is great," Keith explains. "But some of the feedback I got was from people who are more drawn toward stories, and they don't feel that the display is all that engaging. I need to find some accounts of individuals or battalions who fought in these battles so that I can tell their stories, not just list off the number who died." He then talks through some of the strategies he might use to find first-person accounts and describes initial ideas about where he could insert these narratives in the display.

Following Keith's example, students break up into teams to discuss their own feedback. Their discussions are guided by a set of four questions written on the board that ask students to compare their goals for the display with the observations of the reviewers and then to develop an action plan for making changes:

Peer Critique Analysis

1. Goals: What did you want to communicate through your museum display?
2. Feedback analysis: What does the feedback tell you about what you actually communicated?
3. Proposed changes: What changes do you plan to make to your display? (Be specific.)
4. Action plan: Who is responsible for which revisions? When will your revisions be completed?

After much debate, Jena, Seth, and Kayley decide that they need to adjust their display's title from "Weapons of World War I" to "The New Weapons of War," a relatively small change but one that provides a direction for their work. They also add an overall introduction as well as a paragraph after the description of each

Figure 5.8. Museum feedback form.

Museum Feedback Form

Welcome to our display on the Weapons of World War I. We look forward to hearing your feedback -- Jena, Kayley, & Seth

I learned...
What did you learn from our display?

That there were lots of different types of weapons in World War I.
There was lots of information about how each weapon worked and how many people died.
The information about poison gas was particularly disturbing.

I wonder...
What questions did our display raise for you?

I know we talked in class about the new weapons in World War I, but I didn't see a lot of information about which weapons were new.
Were they all new? How were they different from earlier wars?

Suggestions...
What suggestions do you have for the design and content of our display?

It seems like there is a lot of information here but I don't really see how all of the facts connect. I think if I was a World War I scholar or a weapons geek I might like all of the data but for me it just seems like a lot of numbers. It might be helpful to use headings or graphics to show how the information connects.

Submit

Never submit passwords through Google Forms.

weapon describing how the weapon is different from those of previous years and the impact of this weapon both strategically and in human terms. Finally, at Seth's suggestion, they decide to create a graphic that compares the weapons, death tolls, and battle strategies of the French Revolution and World War I to communicate more visually the impact of the new technology.

These changes will require significant attention as these students build the historical knowledge required to more effectively communicate their broader understanding. Students will need to return to their textbooks, find new sources to fill in gaps, and redesign their site. This is work that most teenagers are loathe to do, especially since their curriculum often seems more interested in covering and completing rather than genuinely developing rich understanding. These students, however, respond to the challenge. "When we first do a peer critique, it is really hard to hear the feedback," Jena admits.

> But then you think about it and you realize that some of the feedback is really true and some of the suggestions are helpful. It can be hard to go back to the books if you feel like you've already finished something, but I always learn something new. It makes me wonder how much I miss in my other classes when I only have to read something once and then take the test. I feel like I'm going to remember the things I learn here a lot longer because I've gone over it multiple times and have to keep working to improve our work.

Teaching for Real: Tips for Successful Implementation

So where to begin? While in the midst of putting finishing edits to this book, I met up with a teacher friend for coffee. She asked what I was up to and I described the book, the classrooms I'd observed, and the concept of real-world literacies. As I spoke, her eyes grew wide. "That all sounds great," she observed. "I love the concept, but I don't know how to make that work in my classroom. I have thirty or more kids in each period and many of them are English language learners. My principal is freaking out about Common Core and what that is going to mean for our school's standardized test scores. And even though I studied biology in college, I never actually worked as a biologist. I don't know where I would begin."

Each of these concerns is completely valid. And the strength of my friend's reaction over what was supposed to be a relaxing cup of coffee represents the level of stress and pressure that many of us teachers feel. We all want to give our students meaningful, engaging learning opportunities, but so many factors seem to work against us.

Following are five tips for navigating the obstacles to implementing real-world literacy practices in real-world classrooms. These are the ideas I shared with my friend over a second cup of coffee (and a cookie—everything is better with a cookie). They helped her rethink how she might begin to reframe her teaching to integrate a real-world literacy approach. I share them here in the hope that they will be helpful to you as well.

Tip #1: Explore the literacy practices of your discipline

Many of us went into teaching immediately after college, and although we likely have strong content knowledge, we may be missing an understanding of the current practices of professionals in our disciplines. While researching the portraits of the nurses, engineers, mechanics, lawyers, and other professionals who populate the vignettes at the beginning of the chapters in this book, I learned a tremendous amount about literacy expectations outside the walls of the classroom. Reading, writing, listening, and speaking demands in the work world have certainly changed in the twenty years since I graduated from college!

If the whole concept of disciplinary literacy still seems a bit fuzzy, I encourage you to find opportunities to investigate the literacy practices of professionals in fields connected with your discipline. This can be as simple as asking friends, neighbors, or college roommates to share how they use reading or writing in their work. I posted a Facebook request for ideas about literacy in the workplace and got some fantastic responses that led to more in-depth phone and email conversations. Your investigation could also take the form of attending a workshop or participating in an internship that immerses you in the discipline. These opportunities are especially prevalent for teachers in the STEM disciplines, where engineering, computer science, and biotechnology companies and government agencies offer programs for teachers to become an "engineer for a day" or fellowships to participate in grant-based research projects. Another option: subscribe to an online journal, join a listserv, or follow blogs or tweets posted by professionals in your discipline. Or take a course designed for working professionals in your discipline through a university extension program, or explore one of the massive open online courses (MOOCs) available free through edX, Coursera, and Udacity, among others. Many of these courses offer an applied approach to the disciplines with literacy experiences that reflect the demands of the field. You may be able to count the course toward continuing education requirements for your teaching credential. And you'll be in class alongside professionals whom you can tap to learn more about the literacy demands of their work.

Reaching out to other professionals and investigating literacy practices in related disciplines requires effort. But in my experience, the benefits are very much worth the relatively small amount of time and energy invested. I've come away from my conversations with colleagues in other fields inspired by the work they are doing and excited to engage my students in similar learning experiences. Some of my best problem-based learning ideas have germinated from casual discussions with friends as they share what is happening in their workplaces. And the connections made through these conversations can often be incredibly helpful later on when you are looking for experts to come talk with your students or for community members to serve on presentation panels.

Once you begin thinking through the lens of applied disciplinary literacies, you'll be amazed how many sources of information and inspiration you'll find around you. You can hardly pick up a magazine or scan through a news website without seeing stories that point to disciplinary-driven literacy practices in real-world contexts. The information is there; we just need to learn how to look for it.

Tip #2: Look for connections across competing demands

If the concept of disciplinary literacy is simply "one more thing" on top of state-based content standards, Common Core State Standards, district benchmark assessments, textbook pacing guides, and Advanced Placement (AP) test requirements, it will never make it into your classroom practice. As teachers we have so many different individuals and agencies telling us what to do that it seems nearly impossible to meet all of the various requirements. At their foundation, however, all of those external mandates want the same thing we do: students who graduate from high school with the skills and knowledge needed to succeed in college and the workforce and to be informed citizens in the communities in which they live.

Rather than look at each mandate individually, we need to take a collective step back to consider what these mandates have in common and how we can work from these common goals to build meaningful instruction. In the previous chapters, text boxes highlight some of the connections between the real-world literacy practices described in the chapter and CCSS expectations. Further synchronicity is clear when you drill down into the Common Core State Standards as articulated for specific disciplines and grade levels. Across all of the CCSS literacy standards there is an expectation that literacy instruction be responsive to the specific demands of the discipline and that through their reading, writing, listening, and speaking, students develop critical thinking and analysis skills appropriate to the discipline.

Similar connections can be found beyond the CCSS, e.g., in state-based content standards, AP requirements, and, in many cases, district benchmarks. When I do professional development work with teachers in California around state content standards in history or science, we often spend time considering the critical thinking skills that are implicit (though not always spelled out explicitly) in the standards. We note the use of language such as "students will *analyze* specific events in the founding of the nation" and consider how this is different from "students will *enumerate* specific events in the founding of the nation." This seems like a small point, but calling attention to the distinction between *analyze* and *enumerate* opens up a space to move beyond a focus on teaching facts and allows us to consider how we can teach critical analysis through reading and responding to primary and secondary source documents relevant to this time period, an approach directly supported by most standards in history and the social sciences these days. Over the past decade or so, AP course outlines have similarly shifted to increase their emphasis on encouraging disciplinary thinking and promoting discipline-based practices. This shift is evidenced through the increased use of free response questions and document-based questions (DBQs) on the AP exams. To be successful on these kinds of questions, students need to be very familiar with disciplinary reading and writing practices, practices that align across multiple content literacy standards.

Of course, it would be nice if some of the makers of mandates would lead the efforts to look for commonality across the various demands placed on teachers. But I won't hold my breath waiting for this to happen. As teachers we are the intercessors between the mandates and our students—whatever the mandates happen to be. If we allow the mandates to overwhelm us, then our students will suffer from a fractured curriculum that jumps from one set of demands to another. On the other hand, if we look for commonalities, we can take ownership of the instruction and design learning experiences that respond to these common goals in a manner that is meaningful and relevant for our students.

Tip #3: Adapt practices to respond to the needs of your students

Although the concept of disciplinary literacy applies to all students, the particulars of classroom implementation will vary in response to the strengths, needs, and interests of your students. Variation can be as simple as adapting the length of a writing assignment, being more explicit in teaching students the academic language needed to engage in listening and speaking activities, choosing a text with an easier reading level, or even adapting a discipline-based text to make it more accessible for students. During a presentation I attended a few years ago, Stanford history education professor Sam Wineburg acknowledged that many in the academic history community object to adapting primary source documents to make them more readable for students. But he vigorously defended the practice, arguing that if the choice is between reading an adapted document and not reading primary source documents at all, he would choose the former every time.

The key here is that students have the opportunity to *approximate* real-world professionals. We are not expecting that all tenth-grade chemistry students, for example, will read, write, and talk exactly as a professional chemist would. Rather, the goal is to immerse tenth-grade chemistry students in learning experiences that reflect the literacy norms of the discipline so that they can learn to approximate the ways of thinking of the discipline.

A helpful analogy might be the concept of an apprenticeship. Back in the Middle Ages, if someone was apprenticing to become a carpenter or a blacksmith, he wasn't immediately given all of the tools and expected to make a chair or a horseshoe from start to finish. But he also wasn't told that he could only hear lectures or read textbooks about the trades or that he needed to wait until he passed all the tests before he could do hands-on work. Instead, he was given opportunities to approximate the work of the master, initially learning to use the tools on a scrap piece of wood or metal and then progressively working his way up to more challenging tasks with the guidance and support of the master craftsman. We need to offer our students similarly responsive opportunities to approximate the work of professionals in our disciplines, recognizing potential limitations and scaffolding the learning experiences as needed but making the work hands-on and guiding them toward mastery.

Tip #4: Collaborate with colleagues

Investigating discipline-based literacy practices, thinking about connections with the CCSS and state-based content standards, designing authentic literacy experiences for your classroom—all of these efforts take time and energy. If at all possible, don't go it alone! Connect with like-minded teacher colleagues who want to do similar work. Collaborate in your investigations and your lesson designs. Share samples of student work, problem-solve together, and work with one another to identify community resources and disciplinary materials to bring into the classroom.

My experiences in the classroom were always enriched when I was part of a professional learning community (PLC). These were my teacher friends and colleagues who I planned with, cried with, and celebrated with. Together our energy and creativity was exponentially greater than the sum of our individual parts. Bouncing ideas off of one another during the planning process allowed us to brainstorm outside of the box and then transform sometimes wacky seed ideas into grounded, authentic, discipline-based projects. Bringing in samples of student work from each of our classes helped us to see strengths in our own students that we might not have noticed initially and to think strategically about how to respond to areas of concern. We piggybacked off of one another for guest speakers, rubric designs, and reading materials. Perhaps most important, my PLC provided a reflective space for conversations around the core questions of teaching: Is what I'm doing having an impact on students' learning? How can I improve my practice? What do my students need to be successful? How can I help them get there?

Collegial collaboration and PLCs can take many forms. I've been fortunate to work with schools that dedicate time within the school schedule for collaboration between grade-level or department-based teams, a true gift for busy teachers. But I've also experienced informal collaborative relationships that took place outside of any formal arrangement, sometimes within the discipline and sometimes across disciplines. In my own practice, one of the most productive and meaningful collaborations was with two colleagues who worked down the hall. They taught different grade levels and subject areas than I did, but we shared a common desire to find ways to make learning meaningful for kids. Our conversations provided inspiration and encouragement, as well as practical ideas for growing hands-on learning in the classroom.

If your school already implements teaming or has a PLC structure in place, use it! Ask questions and propose ideas that will push the group toward integrating real-world literacy practices. Share some of the vignettes from this book, encourage the group to take a hard look at the CCSS and the state-based content standards, and think together about how to apply the concepts in these documents to the particulars of your classrooms. If your school doesn't have teaming in place (or if the team isn't working for you), find ways to create your own professional learning community. Seek out like-minded teachers who want to explore literacies of the discipline in greater depth. Invite these colleagues to share ideas and plan together over a cup of coffee and a cookie (after all, everything is better with a cookie!). Use networks in and out of your school or district, including state and local chapters of professional organizations such as the National Council of Teachers of English, the National Science Teachers Association, the National Council of Teachers of Mathematics, or the National Council for the Social Studies. My "go to" organization is my local chapter of the National Writing Project. We come from different schools, disciplines, and grade levels, but I always find inspiration and get ideas from my colleagues there. And with the ubiquity of Facebook, Twitter, and other social media, I can stay in touch and continue the collaboration even when distance and time prevent us from meeting face to face.

Tip #5: Start small

The examples found in this book describe the work of expert teachers, many of whom have been engaged in literacies of the disciplines for years. Collectively, these examples are intended to provide a vision of what real-world literacy can look like in the classroom. They are not, however, intended to be a recipe nor a mandate. If you are just beginning to consider how to integrate real-world literacy practices into your classroom, or if you are in a context that makes the integration of these approaches challenging, don't feel that you have an all-or-nothing choice.

Start small. Choose one or two discipline-based readings to include alongside the textbook. Invite a professional from a field related to your content area to come share their literacy experiences with your class. Reframe an existing writing or presentation assignment so that it is oriented toward an outside audience. Provide opportunities for students to critique their work and revise before they submit for a final grade. Early forays into this work don't need to be (and probably shouldn't be) large-scale interdisciplinary projects; start with a single lesson, a new assignment, or a brainstorming session with a friend.

And don't expect perfection. Each of the teachers profiled in this book will tell you that they have had many days when their plans just didn't seem to work: The great article from the scientific journal that turned out to be much too hard for students to read. The thoughtfully designed Socratic seminar discussion that fell completely flat when students refused to talk. The fantastic project that fell apart two days before presentations for an audience that included the superintendent. We have all been there. We've all had lessons that didn't work, projects that never took off, and students we struggled to connect with. Some of my failures have been, in the words of a former student, "epic." But in the same way that we need to allow students to learn from their mistakes, we need to give ourselves permission to make mistakes, reflect on what we've learned from them, and pick ourselves up and try again.

If a lesson plan or activity doesn't work the first time, it doesn't mean you should abandon your efforts to integrate more disciplinary literacy into the classroom. Keep at it: change the way you introduce the material; provide a bit more scaffolding support; or just try the same lesson a week or two later, knowing that sometimes it takes a little practice to adjust to something new. And don't be afraid to ask the students for their input. We often forget that they've become "experts" during their eight or more years of classroom observation in what works and what doesn't. When I'm not sure where to go next, some of my best solutions have come from explaining our learning goals to the students and then listening to their ideas.

When I was writing my first book and obsessing over the structure of a chapter or the wording of a paragraph, a good friend and fellow teacher looked me in the eye and told me, "It doesn't have to be perfect to be effective." I've repeated that phrase often to myself, to my colleagues, and to the preservice teachers in my university courses. It applies to teaching as well as to writing. So often we get hung up

on all the reasons why we can't do something: it's not the right time, I don't have
the right resources, I'm not sure I have the ability, etc. But teaching doesn't have to
be perfect to be effective. If we wait to have more time, resources, or abilities, we
may never get started. We know that the demands for twenty-first-century reading, writing, listening, and speaking skills are real. We know that our graduates
are too often underprepared to meet those demands. And we know that literacy
competence is a key factor in determining college, career, and community success.
We can't afford to wait. Instruction doesn't have to be perfect to be effective. Find
ways to integrate real-world literacy into the classroom today.

Notes

1. The names of students, teachers, and schools in this book have been changed to protect their privacy.

2. Scott's class publishes his books with Blurb, an on-demand publisher that provides free software that students use for the layout and formatting of the text. The pricing structure, along with donations from the school PTA and booster clubs, keeps costs low and makes the purchase of a text affordable for both the school and individual students.

Annotated Bibliography

Books

Berger, Ron
An Ethic of Excellence: Building a Culture of Craftsmanship with Students.
Portsmouth: Heinemann, 2003.

This thin volume has attracted a dedicated following of outstanding educators. Ron Berger draws on his experience as a veteran teacher, consultant, and chief academic officer at Expeditionary Learning (http://elschools.org) to share a vision for creating schools and classrooms that demand excellence. Berger offers practical tips for helping students to create "beautiful work" and explains that in doing so we not only deepen students' learning but we also nurture their independence and self-worth.

Meier, Deborah
The Power of Their Ideas: Lessons for America from a Small School in Harlem.
Boston: Beacon, 2002.

This book is a classic in the discussion of school reform. Deborah Meier describes the successes of Central Park East Secondary School (CPESS) as a counternarrative to the standardized test–driven approach to school improvement. A leader in the small schools movement, Meier advocates for authentic learning experiences that respond to real-world problems, individual student personalization, and an approach to assessment that focuses on mastery. Grounded in research and supported by multiple detailed examples from CPESS, the school where Meier served as founder and principal, this book is both personal and visionary.

National Writing Project, and Carl Nagin
Because Writing Matters: Improving Student Writing in Our Schools.
San Francisco: Jossey-Bass, 2006.

Published by the National Writing Project, this book shares relevant research as well as practical strategies for effectively teaching writing in K–12 classrooms. The book offers advice for increasing both the quantity and the quality of writing and includes sections on the use of technology, responding to the needs of English language learners, and assessment and standardized testing.

Steinberg, Adria
Real Learning, Real Work: School-to-Work as High School Reform.
New York: Routledge, 1997.

Although Steinberg's text was written nearly two decades ago, the ideas and concerns remain relevant today. Steinberg argues that our schools too often disconnect young people, who may be bright and engaged outside of school, from relevant, meaningful work in the classroom. Using detailed classroom portraits as examples of what is possible, Steinberg lays out clear principles for creating relevant learning environments through project-based learning, community connections, and work-based learning programs.

Wiggins, Grant, and Jay McTighe
Understanding by Design. 2nd ed.
Alexandria: ASCD, 2005.

A widely read text about instructional design that crosses grade levels and disciplines, this practical guide for designing instruction prioritizes conceptual understanding and authentic assessment. Wiggins and McTighe encourage "backward design," starting with the establishment of learning outcomes, then developing final assessments that measure the learning outcomes, before creating the learning experiences that support student growth. The book includes lots of classroom examples and graphic organizers to help teachers through the design process.

Zhao, Yong
***Catching Up or Leading the Way: American
Education in the Age of Globalization.***
Alexandria: ASCD, 2009.

This is a fascinating book that compares American
and Chinese education policies in order to shine
light on the disconnect between the need for edu-
cating creative, independent thinkers and many
of the current test-driven reforms in the United
States. Zhao shares accounts from his own school-
ing as a student in China as well as experiences as
a parent of children in the US education system to
contextualize data from K–12 and higher education in the United States and abroad. At a time
when international studies are routinely cited
as evidence of America's failings, Zhao's book
provides an engaging and thought-provoking perspective on what we have historically done "right"
and raises important questions about our future.

Websites

Buck Institute for Education (www.bie.org)

The Buck Institute for Education is a research and
advocacy organization that focuses on project-
based learning. Their website provides a range of
materials for educators, including videos of sample
projects, research data, and instructional guides.
They also publish a PBL Toolkit series that is
particularly useful. At this time, there are three
editions—PBL Starter Kit, PBL in the Elementary Grades, and PBL for 21st Century Success.
Each includes step-by-step information about how
to design, teach, and assess projects that are responsive to the expectations of your discipline and
the demands of your classroom. Helpful planning
guides and classroom examples are included.

ConnectEd (www.connectedcalifornia.org/linked_
learning)

ConnectEd, the California Center for Career and
College, is a research and advocacy organization
that focuses on building linked learning pathways
that connect school with real-world work and

prepare students for success in college, career, and
community. Their website offers helpful videos,
instructional guides, research reports, and school-
site examples. Focused primarily on California
and including a strong emphasis on STEM, the
information has relevance that extends beyond
these areas to all states and disciplines.

Edutopia (www.edutopia.org/project-based-
learning)

Edutopia, founded by filmmaker George Lucas,
aims to share evidence-based K–12 learning strategies that empower teachers to improve education. Project-based learning (PBL) is one of their
six core strategies. The website includes a com-
pilation of videos, articles, research reports, and
advice from experts on how to implement PBL
in K–12 schools. Materials are compiled from a
range of sites and are very user-friendly, providing
great resources for professional learning communities, professional development workshops, and
collaborative teaching teams.

High Tech High Charter Schools (www.high
techhigh.org)

The High Tech High (HTH) network of charter
schools was launched by a coalition of business
leaders and educators as a single high school in
2000. In the years since, the schools have been
remarkably successful and have attracted significant attention from other educators, reformers,
parents, and policymakers nationally and interna-
tionally. Project-based learning, personalization,
and real-world connections are at the heart of the
work at HTH schools. The HTH website has a
wealth of materials describing the school, its principles, and protocols used by teachers and students
and includes examples of specific projects that are
searchable by grade level and content area. Additionally, HTH's Graduate School of Education
publishes a journal, *Unboxed*, that includes both
classroom portraits of student learning and more
research-focused articles.

Partnership for 21st Century Skills (www.p21.org)
A coalition of educators, policymakers, and business leaders, the Partnership for 21st Century Skills was founded in 2002 to kick-start a national conversation about twenty-first-century readiness and K–12 education. They provide tools and materials for teachers, policymakers, and parents, with a focus on defining, understanding, and implementing twenty-first-century skills. Of particular interest is their learning framework, which couples learning and innovation skills (the 4 *C*s—critical thinking, communication, collaboration, and creativity) with life and career skills, information, media and technology skills, and core subjects to represent desired student learning outcomes.

Reports on Literacy

Multiple reports on literacy are cited in this book. Here I've listed several of my favorites. These are worth an additional read if you are interested in more information about literacy challenges and opportunities presented by the status quo contrasted with future demands. All are available online. For the most recent data on literacy and other education measures, the National Center for Education Statistics publishes annual reports on "The Condition of Education": http://nces.ed.gov/programs/coe/.

ACT
Reading between the Lines: What the ACT Reveals about College Readiness and Reading.
Iowa City: ACT, 2006.
www.act.org/research/policymakers/pdf/reading_report.pdf

Biancarosa, Gina, and Catherine E. Snow
Reading Next—A Vision for Action and Research in Middle and High School Literacy: A Report to the Carnegie Corporation of New York. 2nd ed.
Washington, DC: Alliance for Excellent Education, 2006.

http://carnegie.org/fileadmin/Media/Publications/PDF/ReadingNext.pdf

Casner-Lotto, Jill, and Mary Wright Benner
Are They Really Ready to Work? Employers' Perspectives on the Basic Knowledge and Applied Skills of New Entrants to the 21st Century U.S. Workforce.
New York: The Conference Board; Washington, DC: Corporate Voices for Working Families; Washington, DC: Partnership for 21st Century Skills; and Alexandria, VA: Society for Human Resource Management, 2006.
www.p21.org/storage/documents/FINAL_REPORT_PDF09-29-06.pdf

Graham, Steve, and Dolores Perin
Writing Next: Effective Strategies to Improve Writing of Adolescents in Middle and High Schools—A Report to the Carnegie Corporation of New York.
Washington, DC: Alliance for Excellent Education, 2007.
www.all4ed.org/files/WritingNext.pdf

National Commission on Writing
Writing: A Ticket to Work . . . Or a Ticket Out: A Survey of Business Leaders.
New York: College Board, 2004.
www.collegeboard.com/prod_downloads/writingcom/writing-ticket-to-work.pdf

Peter D. Hart Research Associates/Public Opinion Strategies
Rising to the Challenge: Are High School Graduates Prepared for College and Work?
Washington, DC: Achieve, 2005.
www.achieve.org/files/pollreport_0.pdf

TED Talks

The following TED Talks all respond to the idea of learning by doing. If you haven't watched Ken

Robinson share his ideas, take a few minutes to enjoy
and share with a colleague!

- www.ted.com/speakers/sir_ken_robinson.html

- www.ted.com/talks/ken_robinson_says_
  schools_kill_creativity.html

- www.ted.com/talks/sir_ken_robinson_bring_
  on_the_revolution.html

- www.ted.com/talks/ken_robinson_changing_
  education_paradigms.html

- www.ted.com/talks/ken_robinson_how_to_
  escape_education_s_death_valley.html

Works Cited

ACT. (2006). *Reading between the lines: What the ACT reveals about college readiness and reading.* Iowa City: Author.

Adelman, C. (2004). *Principal indicators of student academic histories in post-secondary education, 1972–2000.* Washington, DC: US Department of Education, Institute of Education Sciences. Retrieved from http://www2.ed.gov/rschstat/research/pubs/prinindicat/prinindicat.pdf

Alliance for Excellent Education. (2007, April). *Making writing instruction a priority in America's middle and high schools* (Policy Brief). Washington, DC: Author. Retrieved from http://all4ed.org/reports-factsheets/making-writing-instruction-a-priority-in-americas-middle-and-high-schools/

Allington, R. L. (2005). *What really matters for struggling readers: Designing research-based programs* (2nd ed.). Boston, MA: Allyn and Bacon.

Allington, R. L., & Johnston, P. (2001). *Reading to learn: Lessons from exemplary fourth grade classrooms.* New York: Guilford Press.

Andolina, M. W., Jenkins, K., Zukin, C., & Keeter, S. (2003). Habits from home, lessons from school: Influences on youth civic engagement. *PS: Political Science and Politics, 36*(2), 275–80.

Applebee, A. N., & Langer, J. A. (2006). *The state of writing instruction in America's schools: What existing data tell us.* Albany, NY: Center on English Learning and Achievement.

Armbruster, B. B., & Anderson, T. H. (1981). *Content area textbooks* (Reading Education Report No. 23). Champaign, IL: Center for the Study of Reading; Cambridge, MA: Bolt, Beranek, and Newman.

Atwell, N. (1998). *In the middle: New understandings about writing, reading, and learning* (2nd ed.). Portsmouth, NH: Boynton/Cook-Heinemann.

Au, K. H. (2000). A multicultural perspective on policies for improving literacy achievement: Equity and excellence. In M. L. Kamil, P. B. Mosenthal, P. D. Pearson, & R. Barr (Eds.), *Handbook of reading research* (Vol. 3, pp. 835–51). Mahwah, NJ: Erlbaum.

August, D., & Shanahan, T. (2006). *Developing literacy in second-language learners: Report of the National Literacy Panel on Language-Minority Children and Youth.* Mahwah, NJ: Erlbaum.

Avery, P. (2002). Teaching tolerance: What the research tells us. *Social Education, 66*(5), 270–75.

Banchi, H., & Bell, R. (2008). The many levels of inquiry. *Science and Children, 46*(2), 26–29.

Bangert-Drowns, R. L., Hurley, M. M., & Wilkinson, B. (2004). The effects of school-based writing-to-learn interventions on academic achievement: A meta-analysis. *Review of Educational Research, 74*(1), 29–58.

Beach, R., & Myers, J. (2001). *Inquiry-based English instruction: Engaging students in life and literature.* New York: Teachers College Press.

Benitez, M., Davidson, J., & Flaxman, L. (2009). *Small schools, big ideas: The essential guide to successful school transformation.* San Francisco, CA: Jossey-Bass.

Berger, R. (2003). *An ethic of excellence: Building a culture of craftsmanship with students.* Portsmouth, NH: Heinemann.

Berger, R. (2008). Crafting beautiful work. *Unboxed, 1.* Retrieved from http://www.hightechhigh.org/unboxed/issue1/crafting_beautiful_work/

Bergmann, L. S., & Zepernick, J. (2007). Disciplinarity and transfer: Students' perceptions of learning to write. *Writing Program Administration, 31*(1–2), 124–49.

Biancarosa, G., & Snow, C. E. (2006). *Reading next—A vision for action and research in middle and high school literacy: A report to the Carnegie Corporation of New York* (2nd ed.). Washington, DC: Alliance for Excellent Education. Retrieved from http://carnegie.org/fileadmin/Media/Publications/PDF/ReadingNext.pdf

Blau, S. D. (2003). *The literature workshop: Teaching texts and their readers.* Portsmouth, NH: Heinemann.

Boaler, J. (1997). *Experiencing school mathematics: Teaching styles, sex and setting.* Buckingham, UK:

Open University Press.

Bomer, R. (1995). *Time for meaning: Crafting literate lives in middle and high school.* Portsmouth, NH: Heinemann.

Bransford, J. D., Brown, A. L., & Cocking, R. R. (Eds.). (2000). *How people learn: Brain, mind, experience, and school.* Washington, DC: National Academy Press.

Brozo, W. G., & Hargis, C. H. (2003). Taking seriously the idea of reform: One high school's efforts to make reading more responsive to all students. *Journal of Adolescent and Adult Literacy, 47*(1), 14–23.

Bruner, J. S. (1966). *Toward a theory of instruction.* Cambridge, MA: Belknap Press of Harvard University.

Calkins, L. M. (2001). *The art of teaching reading.* New York: Longman.

Carpenter, T. P., Fennema, E., Franke, M. L., Levi, L., & Empson, S. B. (1999). *Children's mathematics: Cognitively guided instruction.* Portsmouth, NH: Heinemann.

Carter, M. (2007). Ways of knowing, doing and writing in the disciplines. *College Composition and Communication, 58*(3), 385–418.

Casner-Lotto, J., & Benner, M. W. (2006). *Are they really ready to work? Employers' perspectives on the basic knowledge and applied skills of new entrants to the 21st century U.S. workforce.* New York: The Conference Board; Washington, DC: Corporate Voices for Working Families; Washington, DC: Partnership for 21st Century Skills; and Alexandria, VA: Society for Human Resource Management.

Cawelti, G. (2004). *Handbook of research on improving student achievement* (3rd ed.). Arlington, VA: Educational Research Service.

Center for Advanced Research and Technology. (2011, January). *A model for success: CART's linked learning program increases college enrollment.* Clovis, CA: Author.

Center on English Learning and Achievement. (2006). *Raising the level of student engagement in higher order talk and writing.* Albany, NY: Author.

Center for Workforce Preparation. (2002). *A chamber guide to improving workplace literacy: Higher skills,* *bottom-line results.* Washington, DC: US Chamber of Commerce, Center for Workforce Preparation.

Childers, P. B. (2007). High school-college collaborations: Making them work. *Across the Disciplines: A Journal of Language, Learning, and Academic Writing, 4.* Retrieved from http://wac.colostate.edu/atd/secondary/column2007.cfm

Coalition for Juvenile Justice. (2001). *Abandoned in the back row: New lessons in education and delinquency prevention.* Washington, DC: Author. Retrieved from http://www.juvjustice.org/sites/default/files/resource-files/resource_122_0.pdf

Coalition of Essential Schools. (n.d.). *The CES common principles.* Retrieved from http://www.essentialschools.org/items/4

Common Core State Standards Initiative. (2012). *English language arts standards.* Retrieved from http://www.corestandards.org/ELA-Literacy

Council of Chief State School Officers, & National Governors Association Center on Best Practices. (2010). *Common core state standards for English language arts and literacy in history/social science, science, and technical subjects* (Appendix A). Washington, DC: Authors.

Deci, E. L. (with Flaste, R.). (1996). *Why we do what we do: Understanding self-motivation.* New York: Penguin.

Dewey, J. (1916). *Democracy and education: An introduction to the philosophy of education.* New York: Macmillan.

Doering, A., Beach, R., & O'Brien, D. (2007). Infusing multimodal tools and digital literacies into an English education program. *English Education, 40*(1), 41–60.

Driscoll, E. (2011, March 4). Um, like, whatever: College grads lack verbal skills. *FoxBusiness.* Retrieved from http://www.foxbusiness.com/personal-finance/2011/03/03/um-like-college-grads-lack-verbal-skills/

Elbow, P. (1994). *Writing for learning—Not just for demonstrating learning.* Retrieved from http://www.oberlin.edu/ctie/Elbow-Learning.pdf

Ericson, B. O. (2001). Reading in high school English classes: An overview. In B. O. Ericson (Ed.), *Teaching reading in high school English classes* (pp. 1–22). Urbana, IL: National Council of Teachers of English.

Fisher, D., & Frey, N. (2007). *Improving adolescent literacy: Content area strategies at work* (2nd ed.). Upper Saddle River, NJ: Prentice Hall.

Fitzgerald, J., & Shanahan, T. (2000). Reading and writing relations and their development. *Educational Psychologist, 35*(1), 39–50.

Forsten, C. (1992). *Teaching thinking and problem solving in math: Strategies, problems, and activities.* New York: Scholastic Professional Books.

Gallagher, K. (2006). *Teaching adolescent writers.* Portland, ME: Stenhouse.

Goulden, R., Nation, P., & Read, J. (1990). How large can a receptive vocabulary be? *Applied Linguistics, 11*(4), 341–63.

Graff, N. (2010). Teaching rhetorical analysis to promote transfer of learning. *Journal of Adolescent and Adult Literacy, 53*(5), 376–85.

Graham, S. (2008). *Effective writing instruction for all students.* Wisconsin Rapids, WI: Renaissance Learning. Retrieved from http://doc.renlearn.com/KMNet/R004250923GJCF33.pdf

Graham, S., & Perin, D. (2007). *Writing next: Effective strategies to improve writing of adolescents in middle and high schools—A report to Carnegie Corporation of New York.* Washington, DC: Alliance for Excellent Education. Retrieved from http://www.all4ed.org/files/WritingNext.pdf

Gutmann, A. (1999). *Democratic education.* Princeton, NJ: Princeton University Press.

Harvey, S., & Goudvis, A. (2007). *Strategies that work: Teaching comprehension for understanding and engagement* (2nd ed.). Portland, ME: Stenhouse.

Heller, R. (2010). In praise of amateurism: A friendly critique of Moje's "call for change" in secondary literacy. *Journal of Adolescent and Adult Literacy, 54*(4), 267–73.

Hess, D. E. (2004). Discussion in the social studies: Is it worth the trouble? *Social Education, 68*(2), 151–55.

Hillocks, G., Jr. (1995). *Teaching writing as reflective practice.* New York: Teachers College Press.

Hillocks, G., Jr. (2002). *The testing trap: How state writing assessments control learning.* New York: Teachers College Press.

HireRight, Inc. (2011, August). *Employment screening benchmarking report.* Irvine, CA: Author.

Hoachlander, G., Stearns, R. J., & Studier, C. (2008, January). *Expanding pathways: Transforming high school education in California.* Berkeley, CA: ConnectEd: California Center for College and Career.

Jarrett, D. (2000). Open-ended problem solving: Weaving a web of ideas. *Northwest Education Quarterly, 1*(1), 1–7.

Jensen, E. (2005). *Teaching with the brain in mind* (2nd ed.). Alexandria, VA: Association for Supervision and Curriculum Development.

Joftus, S. (2002, September). *Every child a graduate: A framework for an excellent education for all middle and high school students.* Washington, DC: Alliance for Excellent Education.

Kamil, M. L. (2003, November). *Adolescents and literacy: Reading for the 21st century.* Washington, DC: Alliance for Excellent Education.

Keene, E. O., & Zimmerman, S. (2007). *Mosaic of thought: The power of comprehension strategy instruction* (2nd ed.). Portsmouth, MA: Heinemann.

Knipper, K. J., & Duggan, T. J. (2006). Writing to learn across the curriculum: Tools for comprehension in content area classes. *The Reading Teacher, 59*(5), 462–70.

Lattimer, H. (2010). *Reading for learning: Using discipline-based texts to build content knowledge.* Urbana, IL: National Council of Teachers of English.

Lattimer, H., & Riordan, R. (2011). Project-based learning engages students in meaningful work. *Middle School Journal, 43*(2), 18–23.

Lyon, G. R. (2002). Reading development, reading difficulties, and reading instruction: Educational and public health issues. *Journal of School Psychology, 40*(1), 3–6.

Manpower Group. (2011). *Talent shortage survey results, 2011.* Retrieved from https://candidate.manpower.com/wps/wcm/connect/6ecffb80470e244d9ac3da4a926374bc/2011+Talent+Shortage+Survey_A4_lores.pdf?MOD=AJPERES

Markham, T., Larmer, J., & Ravitz, J. (2003). *Project based learning handbook: A guide to standards-focused project based learning for middle and high school teachers.* Novato, CA: Buck Institute for Education.

Marzano, R. J., Pickering, D. J., & Pollock, J. E. (2001). *Classroom instruction that works: Research-*

based strategies for increasing student achievement. Alexandria, VA: Association for Supervision and Curriculum Development.

McManus, S. (2008). *Attributes of effective formative assessment.* Washington, DC: Council of Chief State School Officers. Retrieved from http://www.ncpublicschools.org/docs/accountability/educators/fastattributes04081.pdf

Meier, D. (2002). *The power of their ideas: Lessons for America from a small school in Harlem.* Boston, MA: Beacon.

Meltzer, J. (with Smith, N. C., & Clark, H.). (2002). *Adolescent literacy resources: Linking research and practice.* Providence, RI: Northeast and Islands Regional Educational Laboratory at Brown University; South Hampton, NH: Center for Resource Management.

Moore, D. W., Bean, T. W., Birdyshaw, D., & Rycik, J. A. (1999). *Adolescent literacy: A position statement for the commission on adolescent literacy of the International Reading Association.* Newark, DE: International Reading Association.

National Association of Colleges and Employers. (2012). *Job outlook 2013.* Bethlehem, PA: Author.

National Association of Manufacturers, Andersen, & Center for Workforce Success. (2001). *The skills gap 2001: Manufacturers confront persistent skills shortages in an uncertain economy.* Retrieved from http://www.themanufacturinginstitute.org/~/media/624B19FCA94E457AA1AF29FDF399652B/2001_Skills_Gap_Report.pdf

National Commission on Writing. (2003, April). *The neglected "R": The need for a writing revolution.* New York: College Board.

National Commission on Writing. (2004, September). *Writing: A ticket to work…Or a ticket out: A survey of business leaders.* New York: College Board. Retrieved from http://www.collegeboard.com/prod_downloads/writingcom/writing-ticket-to-work.pdf

National Council of Teachers of English. (2011). *Literacies of disciplines: A policy research brief.* Retrieved from http://www.ncte.org/library/NCTEFiles/Resources/Journals/CC/0211-sep2011/CC0211Policy.pdf

National Council of Teachers of English. (2012).

Reading instruction for all students: A policy research brief. Retrieved from http://www.ncte.org/library/NCTEFiles/Resources/Journals/CC/0221-sep2012/Chron0221PolicyBrief.pdf

National Writing Project, & Nagin, C. (2006). *Because writing matters: Improving student writing in our schools.* San Francisco, CA: Jossey-Bass.

New London Group. (2000). A pedagogy of multiliteracies: Designing social futures. In B. Cope & M. Kalantzis (Eds.), *Multiliteracies: Literacy learning and the design of social futures* (pp. 9–37). New York: Routledge.

Nichols, M. (2006). *Comprehension through conversation: The power of purposeful talk in the reading workshop.* Portsmouth, NH: Heinemann.

Nichols, M. (2008). *Talking about text: Guiding students to increase comprehension through purposeful talk.* Huntington Beach, CA: Shell Education.

Nichols, M. (2009). *Expanding comprehension with multigenre text sets.* New York: Scholastic.

Nystrand, M. (with Gamoran, A., Kachur, R., & Prendergast, C.). (1997). *Opening dialogue: Understanding the dynamics of language and learning in the English classroom.* New York: Teachers College Press.

Nystrand, M., Wu, L. L., Gamoran, A, Zeiser, S., & Long, D. A. (2003). Questions in time: Investigating the structure and dynamics of unfolding classroom discourse. *Discourse Processes, 35*(2), 135–98.

O'Brien, D. G., Stewart, R. A., & Moje, E. B. (1995). Why content area literacy is difficult to infuse into the secondary school: Complexities of curriculum, pedagogy, and school culture. *Reading Research Quarterly, 30*(3), 442–63.

Parker, W. C. (2003). *Teaching democracy: Unity and diversity in public life.* New York: Teachers College Press.

Partnership for 21st Century Skills. (2011). *Framework for 21st century learning.* Retrieved from http://www.p21.org/storage/documents/1.__p21_framework_2-pager.pdf

Pautler, A. J., Jr. (1998, December). *Workforce education: Issues for the new century.* Paper presented at the American Vocational Association Convention, New Orleans, LA.

Peter D. Hart Research Associates/Public Opinion

Strategies. (2005, February). *Rising to the challenge: Are high school graduates prepared for college and work? A study of recent high school graduates, college instructors, and employers.* Washington, DC: Achieve.

Piaget, J. (1971). *Biology and knowledge: An essay on the relations between organic regulations and cognitive processes* (B. Walsh, Trans.). Chicago: University of Chicago Press.

Postman, N., & Weingartner, C. (1971). *Teaching as a subversive activity.* New York: Dell.

Pucel, D. J. (1998, May). *The changing role of vocational education and the comprehensive high school.* Paper presented at the International Symposium on Comprehensive High School Education, Taipei, Taiwan.

Resnick, L. B. (1999). Making America smarter. *Education Week Century Series, 18*(40): 38–40.

Rex, L., Green, J., Dixon, C., & Santa Barbara Classroom Discourse Group. (1998). Critical issues: What counts when context counts? The uncommon "common" language of literacy research. *Journal of Literacy Research, 30*(3), 405–33.

Rief, L. (2007). Writing: Commonsense matters. In K. Beers, R. E. Probst, & L. Rief (Eds.), *Adolescent literacy: Turning promise into practice* (pp. 189–208). Portsmouth, NH: Heinemann.

Robinson, K. (Speaker). (2010, February). *Ted talk: Bring on the learning revolution!* Retrieved from http://www.ted.com/talks/sir_ken_robinson_bring_on_the_revolution.html

Rose, M. (1989). *Lives on the boundary.* New York: Penguin.

Rothman, R. (2012). A common core of readiness. *Educational Leadership, 69*(7), 10–15.

Russell, D. R. (2001). Where do the naturalistic studies of WAC/WID point? A research review. In S. H. MacLeod, E. Miraglia, M. Soven, & C. Thaiss (Eds.), *WAC for the new millennium: Strategies for continuing writing-across-the-curriculum programs* (pp. 259–98). Urbana, IL: National Council of Teachers of English.

Schuster, L., & Anderson, N. C. (2005). *Good questions for math teaching: Why ask them and what to ask, Grades 5–8.* Sausalito, CA: Math Solutions Publications.

Shanahan, T. (2004). Overcoming the dominance of communication: Writing to think and to learn. In T. L. Jetton & J. A. Dole (Eds.). *Adolescent literacy research and practice* (pp. 59–73). New York: Guilford.

Short, K., Schroeder, J., Kauffman, G., & Kaser, S. (2005). Thoughts from the editors. *Language Arts, 82*(3), 167.

Simon, K. G. (2001). *Moral questions in the classroom: How to get kids to think deeply about real life and their schoolwork.* New Haven, CT: Yale University Press.

Sizer, T. R., & Sizer, N. F. (2000). *The students are watching: Schools and the moral contract.* Boston, MA: Beacon Press.

Snow, C. E., & Biancarosa, G. (2003). *Adolescent literacy and the achievement gap: What do we know and where do we go from here?* New York: Carnegie Corporation of New York.

Soep, E. (2006). Critique: Assessment and the production of learning. *Teachers College Record, 108*(4), 748–77.

Sousa, D. A. (2001). *How the brain learns: A classroom teacher's guide* (2nd ed.). Thousand Oaks, CA: Corwin Press.

Sperling, M., & Freedman, S. W. (2001). Research on writing. In V. Richardson (Ed.), *Handbook of research on teaching* (4th ed., pp. 370–89). Washington, DC: American Educational Research Association.

Strobel, J., & van Barneveld, A. (2009). When is PBL more effective? A meta-synthesis of meta-analyses comparing PBL to conventional classrooms. *Interdisciplinary Journal of Problem-based Learning, 3*(1), 44–58.

Strong, S. G. (2009). *How do students experience open-ended math problems? An Action Research Project* (Unpublished master's thesis). High Tech High Graduate School of Education, San Diego, CA. Retrieved from http://dp.hightechhigh.org/~sstrong/dptemplate/documents/Action Research/Sarah%20Strong%20Thesis.pdf

Thaiss, C., & Zawacki, T. M. (2006). *Engaged writers and dynamic disciplines: Research on the academic writing life.* Portsmouth, NH: Heinemann.

Torney-Purta, J., Lehmann, R., Oswald, H., &

Schulz, W. (2001). *Citizenship and education in twenty-eight countries: Civic knowledge and engagement at age fourteen.* Amsterdam: International Association for the Evaluation of Educational Achievement.

Tough, P. (2012). *How children succeed: Grit, curiosity, and the hidden power of character.* New York: Houghton Mifflin Harcourt.

US Department of Education, National Center for Education Statistics (1998). *The condition of education 1998.* (NCES 98013). Washington, DC: US Government Printing Office.

US Department of Education, National Center for Education Statistics (2003). *The condition of education 2003* (NCES 2003-067). Washington, DC: US Government Printing Office.

US Department of Education, National Center for Education Statistics (2004). *The condition of education 2004* (NCES 2004-077). Washington, DC: US Government Printing Office.

US Department of Education, National Center for Education Statistics. (2005, December). *A first look at the literacy of America's adults in the 21st century* (NCES 2006-470). Retrieved from http://nces.ed.gov/pubsearch/pubsinfo.asp?pubid=2006470

US Department of Education, National Center for Education Statistics. (2011, November). *The nation's report card: Reading 2011* (NCES 2012-457). Retrieved from http://nces.ed.gov/nations reportcard/pubs/main2011/2012457.asp

US Department of Education, National Center for Education Statistics. (2012a). *The condition of education 2012* (NCES 2012-045). Washington, DC: US Government Printing Office.

US Department of Education, National Center for Education Statistics. (2012b, September). *The nation's report card: Writing 2011* (NCES 2012-470).

Retrieved from http://nces.ed.gov/nations reportcard/pdf/main2011/2012470.pdf

VanSledright, B. A. (2004). What does it mean to think historically…and how do you teach it? *Social Education 68*(3), 230–33.

Vygotsky, L. S. (1962). *Thought and language.* (E. Hanfmann & G. Vakar, trans.). Cambridge: Massachusetts Institute of Technology Press.

Walker, A., & Leary, H. (2009). A problem based learning meta analysis: Differences across problem types, implementation types, disciplines, and assessment levels. *Interdisciplinary Journal of Problem-based Learning, 3*(1), 6–28.

Wiggins, G., & McTighe, J. (2005) *Understanding by design* (2nd ed.). Alexandria, VA: Association for Supervision and Curriculum Development.

Wineburg, S. (2001). *Historical thinking and other unnatural acts: Charting the future of teaching the past.* Philadelphia, PA: Temple University Press.

Wolf, M. K., Crosson, A. C., & Resnick, L. B. (2005). Classroom talk for rigorous reading comprehension instruction. *Reading Psychology, 26*(1), 27–53.

Yetkiner, Z. E., Anderoglu, H., & Capraro, R. M. (2008). *Research summary: Project-based learning in middle grades mathematics.* Retrieved from http://www.ncmle.org/docs/ProjectBased_Math.pdf

Young, A. (2006). *Teaching writing across the curriculum.* Upper Saddle River, NJ: Pearson Prentice Hall.

Zhao, Y. (2009). *Catching up or leading the way: American education in the age of globalization.* Alexandria, VA: Association for Supervision and Curriculum Development.

Zinsser, W. (2001). *On writing well: The classic guide to writing nonfiction* (25th anniversary edition). New York: HarperCollins.

Index

Author

Heather Lattimer is an associate professor of education and chair of the Department of Learning and Teaching in the School of Leadership and Education Sciences at the University of San Diego. A former middle and high school teacher, she holds credentials in three content areas: history/social science, mathematics, and English language arts. Lattimer has previously published four books, including *Thinking through Genre: Units of Study in Reading and Writing Workshops 4–12* (2003) and *Reading for Learning: Using Discipline-Based Texts to Build Content Knowledge* (2010). A nationally recognized speaker and consultant, her scholarly work focuses on secondary literacy, disciplinary literacy, teacher education, and international education. Lattimer has earned degrees from Harvard University, Stanford University, and the University of California, San Diego.

This book was typeset in Janson Text and BotonBQ by
Barbara Frazier.

Typefaces used on the cover include American Typewriter,
Frutiger Bold, Formata Light, and Formata Bold.

The book was printed on 60-lb. White Recycled Offset paper
by Versa Press, Inc.

30% Total Recycled Fiber